ELMHURST PUBLIC LIBRARY

3 1135 02007 2028

MW00345727

629.2275
Dap

VICTORY

MOTORCYCLES | 1998–2017

THE COMPLETE HISTORY OF AN AMERICAN ORIGINAL

MICHAEL DAPPER

AND

LEE KLANCHER

OCTANE PRESS

ELMHURST PUBLIC LIBRARY
125 S. Prospect Avenue
Elmhurst, IL 60126-3298

Octane Press, First Edition
April 2018
© 2017 by Michael Dapper and Lee Klancher

Note that this book includes a complete reprint of:
The Victory Motorcycle, Motorbooks, May 1998, ISBN 978-0760305300

All rights reserved. With the exception of quoting brief passages for the purposes of review,
no part of this publication may be reproduced without prior written permission from the publisher.

ISBN: 978-1-937747-93-0
Library of Congress Control Number: 2017914237

Cover and Interior Design by Tom Heffron
Copy Edited by Aki Neumann
Proofread by Chelsey Clammer

On the cover: 2016 Victory Cross Country owned by Michael Martinez, who added
a few tasteful modifications to a mostly stock machine. *Lee Klancher*

On the endpapers: *Front,* The Octane is a sprinter, made for ripping from corner to corner,
especially when chasing around with a riding buddy. *Back,* Victory Stunt Team riders
Tony Carbajal (shown here) and Joe Dryden rode Octanes for the model's marketing
photo shoot, thus the abundance of rear rubber applied to the pavement. *Victory*

On the frontispiece: A pseudo-silhouetted profile of the Hammer. *Lee Klancher*

On the title page: A Victory Gunner poses on the sand of Daytona Beach. *Victory*

Victory, Victory Motorcycles, and various Victory logos
are trademarks of Polaris Industries Inc.

This book is not licensed or endorsed
by Polaris Industries Inc.

OCTANE
PRESS

octanepress.com
Printed in China

CONTENTS

Building a Legacy

By Mike Song
Senior Staff Industrial Designer for Victory

Reading this history of Victory Motorcycles and reflecting on my 19 years with the brand practically moves me to tears—tears of both joy and sadness. It was a joy to contribute to the brand's incredible history. And of course, it was so sad to learn of Victory's demise. But what a great, great ride we all had.

I came to Polaris in February 1998. It was a major career and life change for me. I had attended design school in my home state of California and was working in automotive design in Southern California. I went to work every day in a plush, highly secure design studio where we safeguarded details about future projects.

With Polaris, I joined Todd Dannenberg as the second member of the fledgling industrial design team. I hadn't been impressed with the look of the original V92C, but I was a motorcycle guy and relished the opportunity to work on Victory motorcycle design. That's why I made the leap and moved to Polaris—and Minnesota, complete with its nasty winters that were new to me.

My original Polaris workspace was a cube that was set among the accounts payable (AP) staff. The AP women could stick their heads into my workspace at any time and check out designs I was working on.

My first Victory designs were the short fenders of the SportCruiser, followed by the saddlebags of the Touring Cruiser. After that, freed up by new General Manager Mark Blackwell and encouraged by Product Manager Gary Laskin, I created the Vegas. We knew we had to create a brand identity and give Victory its own distinctive style. Man, it was exciting for me as a designer to have so much creative freedom. Plus, I was working with a new engineering team that was open to fresh ideas and shared the whole team's desire to build great bikes.

With the Vegas and so many of the Victory models that followed it, we won awards, earned patents, and challenged riders to choose bikes that moved them beyond their retro comfort zone. We created motorcycles that we felt were progressive, modern, and of course great-riding bikes.

Fortunately, thousands of Victory owners shared our passion for the brand and invested their hard-earned money in these bikes. To all of you, I'm grateful. You put Victory on the road and spread the gospel of the brand.

I'll never view Victory as a failure. I view it as an opportunity and a successful challenge to what was comfortable, familiar, and accepted in the motorcycle world.

The Victory business will end, yes, but the history will remain. Victory owners—myself included on my stripped-down Vegas bobber—will keep on riding 'em 'til the wheels fall off.

Victory's ace photographer and videographer, David Shelleny, captured the green Gunner alongside a military vehicle prior to the 2014 Veterans Day Parade in New York City. *Victory*

Victory Motorcycles Changed Our World

By Robert Pandya
Former External Relations Manager for Victory

As the long-time public relations manager for Victory Motorcycles, I take great pride in all that the Victory team did to elevate the conversation on American V-Twins. I believe time will show that the efforts of Victory engineers and marketers and support from the parent company, Polaris, drove the modern shift in the V-Twin scene.

At first, Victory did not have a story—just motorcycles. The products *became* the story. "The Gunny's" challenge to "Ride One and You'll Own One" became the true acid test for many motorcyclists. These motorcycles handled great, and immediately differentiated themselves in a sea of batwing fairings by delivering what many riders were looking for in a modern American motorcycle. Once you rode one, you knew it was good.

The broad market—trained that "retro is the only way to go" by the volume leader out of Milwaukee—simply was not ready for Victory. It is a big loss to see the brand go away. Victory was the catalyst for significant updates in the Harley lineup (though HD would never admit that!), and without Victory Motorcycles' experience, insights, and commitments made early on, the newest generation of Indian motorcycles would never have been able to emerge as the true challenger to Milwaukee iron.

Some say that Indian Motorcycle killed off Victory within Polaris. Given the brutal headwinds in 2009 and the slim American market opportunities that exist for challengers, it's more correct to say that the current American products would not have been as great as they are without Victory Motorcycles leading the effort. Today's market faces big challenges, and it is sad to no longer see Victory in the fight.

The first motorcycle I introduced for the brand was the Vision. It was a love it or hate it machine, which is how I believe many people see Victory itself—a love it or hate it brand. The truth is that it takes real guts to stake a position in the modern motorcycle market; being in some grey zone with middling products will never work. Victory Motorcycles was inspired and developed by engineers and designers who did their job with genuine passion, creativity, and the bold belief that an American motorcycle could not only be different—it could be way better. The catalyst for that revolutionary mission was Mark Blackwell, the former vice president of Victory and a mentor of mine. He is a true hero, as well as Greg Brew and Michael Song, who delivered stunning products that so many engineers worked hard to perfect.

Many times I proudly stood in front of a crowd and called out these talented men and women. It was an honor to be trusted as their spokesperson. Victory Motorcycles had a strong character and soul, as seen in almost every employee who touched the brand. I believe that Victory Motorcycles represents a true spirit of motorcycling in America, and I know I'll be seeing them on the road for decades to come. Victory is a reminder of the durability, innovation, and heart that defines this great country.

Robert Pandya's company, SpokesPeople LLC, managed external Public Relations for Victory Motorcycles and Indian Motorcycle between 2007–2016. He is an avid rider and is shown here on a ride through Big Bend, Texas, in 2012. *Lee Klancher*

INTRODUCTION

Rolling On

By Michael Dapper
Founding Editor of Victory Rider *Magazine*

This is a love story, one with a sad ending. The people who designed, engineered, and built Victory motorcycles, along with the people who sold, bought, and rode them, all loved them. Great bikes, great people, but limited business success.

This book is as accurate a factual account of Victory history as possible. Admittedly, the content reflects a pro-Victory bias.

The first portion of this book was originally published as *The Victory Motorcycle,* in 1998. It is a detailed account of how the first V92C came to exist, and has been out-of-print for many years. We're pleased to bring this key piece of history back to life, along with new content that covers all the models Victory built.

Polaris, Victory's parent company, releases financial data required of a publically held company, but that data has never reflected motorcycle unit production numbers. Thus, Victory production numbers cited here, culled from a variety of sources, are accurate or reasonable approximations to the best of our knowledge.

Other information in this book is based on first-hand observation or participation, or by interviewing or otherwise communicating with company sources.

We were there at Planet Hollywood when Al Unser, Jr., rode the prototype V92C into the room. (And, oddly, as former professional wrestler and future governor of Minnesota, Jesse Ventura, worked the crowd in the hallway outside the restaurant.)

We rode a Victory on the Kyle Petty Charity Ride, to the top of Pikes Peak, on the beach in Daytona, across the Nevada desert, on Manhattan's Fifth Avenue in the Veterans Day parade (and on the sidewalks of NYC), and past the D.C. memorials during Rolling Thunder.

The Victory story is a love story. It's sad, yes, but also inspiring; even with the business shuttered, the bikes and proud owners roll on.

The open road calls as long-time Victory media representative tackles the twisties in the Hill Country near Austin, Texas.
Lee Klancher

CHAPTER 1

The Making of the V92C

Creating and selling a new motorcycle is a daunting challenge. Just ask the folks who tried to revive Excelsior-Henderson. In the 1990s, they raised a lot of venture capital, got the State of Minnesota to support the project because of its job-creation and tax-revenue potential, and built an impressive factory in Belle Plaine, Minnesota. But the EH dream died the inglorious death of yet another failed business after a brief production run.

As the first Victory V92C was ridden out of the Spirit Lake, Iowa, manufacturing facility in the summer of 1998, Victory became the first mass-produced, all-new brand of American motorcycle since the 1940s. According to motorcycle historian and author Jerry H. Hatfield, "The last American motorcycle to enter production was Mustang. Mustang went on the market in 1945 and quit in 1965."

The Mustang was the Rodney Dangerfield of motorcycles. It failed to earn universal respect because of its small (12 inch) wheels, Hatfield said, "but Mustangs came with a three- or four-speed foot-shift transmission and a telescopic fork, and they had plenty of pep up to their top speed of sixty-five to seventy miles per hour. They also had a loud thump-thump exhaust note as good as anything else."

Around 1946, a firm in Pasadena, California, built at least one prototype Vard motorcycle, but that bike never went into production. (Vard, however, subsequently produced aftermarket telescopic forks for Indians and Harley-Davidsons.)

Unlike those failed efforts, Harley-Davidson was the lone American motorcycle manufacturer of long standing to have survived into the twenty-first century. Harley-Davidson continues to dominate the worldwide heavyweight (1000cc and up) cruiser market. Its sales success in the 1990s and early 2000s revved up competition from Japanese brands, but their combined sales numbers have never threatened the reign of the Milwaukee-based market leader.

With so few long-term American motorcycle success stories on record, what made Polaris think it could successfully produce a motorcycle? Plenty—its manufacturing history, engineering talent, business savvy, and loyal Polaris customers.

Polaris has produced recreational vehicles for 61 years. It has the proven engineering talent and production capabilities to design and produce six (so far) distinctly different vehicle lines, as well as

The Victory V92C was developed at the Victory engineering center, originally located near Polaris headquarters in International Falls and later relocated to an industrial park in Osceola, Wisconsin. This is PD-2, an early V92C prototype, photographed at the train station in Osceola. *Lee Klancher*

produce its own engines for most of those vehicles.

Polaris has also proven the corporate leadership needed to forge a successful, profitable path through the '80s, '90s, and into the new century. For this discussion, the executive focus starts with W. Hall Wendel, Jr., who served as chief executive officer from 1981 to 1999. In 1981, Wendel led a group of investors in purchasing Polaris Industries back from Textron, which in 1968 bought the company from the Roseau, Minnesota, ownership group that included two of the company's three founders.

Wendel was at the helm as the company grew, thrived, and diversified. With Victory, it diversified further, entering the on-road business for the first time.

A New Machine

If Polaris had appointed someone other than Matt Parks as general manager of new products, there's a chance this book would be about Victory golf carts or lawnmowers, not motorcycles.

Parks grew up in California with a love of motorcycles. He also loved tinkering with machinery, which led him to the California Polytechnic State University in San Luis Obispo, which offers excellent mechanical engineering courses—and handy access to countless miles of roads that are ripe for spectacular motorcycle rides.

Parks joined Polaris in 1987 as the district sales manager for California, Nevada, and Arizona. Since the company had only recently introduced its ATVs, his territory had a fledgling dealer network and the Polaris brand had low name recognition. Within just a few years, Parks successfully developed the region's dealer network and showed enough promise and potential to be named ATV product manager in February 1992.

His knowledge, attitude, and ability to analyze the businesses in which Polaris was involved impressed management. Once Parks (then in his early 30s) settled into the company's Minnesota headquarters, management—specifically CEO W. Hall Wendel, Jr.,—sought his opinions and had him research prospective acquisitions and business expansions.

"Starting early in '93, for whatever reason, I would be called in and told, 'Take a look at the such-and-such market. Let's look at go-karts or golf carts, or lawn and garden, chainsaws, or whatever,'" Parks recalled in the late 1990s, when *The Victory Motorcycle* was first published. "I would find out about the industry and who the players are, how big it is and whether it's being well-served, its new trends and whatnot, and I'd present these findings to Hall."

But, he said "nothing really came of it." At least not at first.

Polaris CEO W. Hall Wendel, Jr., sits behind Al Unser, Jr., at the Victory's introduction to the press held in Bloomington, Minnesota, on June 26, 1997. Wendel's leadership diversified Polaris with tremendous success. His vision of branching out beyond snowmobiles made possible the bike's introduction at the Mall of America. The launch featured Little Al riding PD-5, an early preproduction bike, into the throng of press packed into the Planet Hollywood restaurant. *Wayne Davis*

Matt Parks looked at everything from go-karts to chainsaws as possible avenues for Polaris. When the results of a 1993 survey showed a high number of Polaris owners were also motorcyclists, Parks and company executives began to seriously consider adding a motorcycle to the Polaris line. Parks is shown at the June 1997 press introduction. *Victory*

He eventually got a second title, that of general manager of new products, which led to some interesting mail.

"I was sent every Hula-Hoop and every Rube Goldberg device from every quack in the country," Parks said. "They'd say, 'This is a new product. We want you to put Polaris on the side and sell it for nineteen dollars and ninety-five cents.' But we *did* get a lot of fun stuff out of it to test."

None of the prospective new ventures panned out or even called for extensive research—that is, until the need arose for a study of the off-road motorcycle market.

"A couple of companies came up for sale in the dirt bike business, the off-road motorcycle business, and we took a look at that," he recalled. "We studied the dirt bike business fairly intensely, then a motorcycle company came to visit us to see if there was an opportunity to distribute their European motorcycles through Polaris.

"That sparked a study of the motorcycle business that uncovered signs of a promising market. Along with the dirt bike research, we did a quick study of the street bike business at that time, and we were kind of interested. We thought, 'You know, this makes some sense.'"

Polaris Owners Light the Spark

Polaris inserted a survey form in a 1993 issue of the company's *Spirit* magazine, which at the time was mailed to more than 300,000 Polaris vehicle owners. The survey measured readers' interest in a wide variety of products, from fishing boats to lawn and garden equipment, to on- and off-road motorcycles. Respondents were asked if they would be interested in buying such products from Polaris.

"Motorcycling did really, really well [in the survey]," Parks said, "so we said, 'Well, this looks interesting, let's take a look, let's get some outside input.' We wanted to see if there was some opportunity in motorcycling, to see if it was a match with Polaris."

Wendel appointed two product managers—Parks and then-snowmobile product manager Bob Nygaard—to conduct further confidential research

Although Polaris officials considered building an off-road motorcycle, a closer look at the market led them to believe the best opportunity existed in the cruiser market. Cruisers were becoming increasingly popular, customers were waiting several years for Harley-Davidsons, and the technology required to be competitive was attainable for a company starting from scratch. *Lee Klancher*

on motorcycles. Parks and Nygaard (both now retired from Polaris) hired two outside firms to assist them in the project. One was the McKenzie Company, one of largest consulting firms in the world. The other was Minneapolis-based advertising executive Jerry Stahl, who had worked on Harley-Davidson advertising campaigns as an ad agency account executive.

Meanwhile, Parks and Nygaard assessed the Polaris sales force, dealer network, service and warranty operation, and the parts, garment, and accessories division.

"We also looked at our customers to see the types of things they were interested in, and whether they would buy a motorcycle from us," Parks said. "We worked on that pretty hard from May until August [1993]—extremely hard—and the upstairs conference room [in the company's suburban Minneapolis headquarters of that era] was turned into our war room. We had our stuff pinned all over the room."

Nygaard said the motorcycle research effort was different from the company's previous diversification projects.

"We had an outside consulting firm [for the Victory project], which we had never done before," Nygaard said. "We didn't do that when we got into ATVs or watercraft. We had high-powered outside consultants. We brought Jerry Stahl in and talked to him. The research was more sophisticated than we did in the past, and another thing is, with motorcycles, you had good [sales] numbers. You had Motorcycle Industry Council [MIC] numbers, you could tell where they were selling, you could see displacement, types of bikes, that kind of thing. And with the watercraft business, nobody knew. We would ask, 'How many watercraft are being built?' Nobody knew."

The Victory research showed there were opportunities for another manufacturer in the cruiser business—particularly if a newcomer were able to fulfill unsatisfied consumer demand for product, features, and performance.

"We focused in on Harley and the Japanese manufacturers and said to ourselves, 'Is Harley vulnerable from any standpoint?' We thought that their costs were high," Nygaard said. "We thought that, based on re-engineering the Harley bike, we could build it for less money. We felt that customers were waiting too long to take delivery of their Harleys and they [H-D] were vulnerable from that standpoint. We could get to market with a bike that we could make money on, and the heavy cruiser end of it was certainly what we wanted to target because that's where the [sales] numbers were, that's where the [profit] margin was. It was the best fit for us in that the Japanese were vulnerable there because they really hadn't been able to tackle Harley because it might look like a Harley, but the real rider knew that it was not an American-made bike from an American manufacturer. We were close [at the time] to being in the domestic engine business and we could build our own U.S. engine, and that gave us a major leg up on the Japanese. We were an American company."

While still serving as the ATV product manager, Parks traveled the country to interview dealers and consumers, attended motorcycle events, and compiled data along with the McKenzie Company and Stahl. Parks and Nygaard provided the company's officers with monthly updates, and presented their conclusions to management in August 1993.

A New Market Opportunity

"The result of the study was, believe it or not, yes—there was a tremendous opportunity in the motorcycle market," Parks said. "It's not the off-road motorcycle market, it's the on-road motorcycle market and the entry point, the best entry point, would be in the cruiser market. Effectively, there was an oligopoly in the motorcycle market. There were just a very few players selling to the motorcycle market, and in the cruiser business, the Japanese were getting stronger and stronger and that entire business was growing, and it appeared there was decent money to be made there."

The manufacturing capabilities and technological know-how required to produce cruisers seemed within Polaris' grasp, Parks said.

"There were fairly long product life cycles and the technology was manageable," he said. "In other words, we weren't making a moon shot here. The technology was certainly advanced and there's good high-end engineering that goes into the product. But we didn't need a Cray supercomputer to do this kind of thing. It's not NASA."

The Name Game

When Polaris staff members began research in 1993 on the possibility of entering the motorcycle business, they needed to keep their work confidential. The project needed a code name so they could refer to it without calling it "the motorcycle project."

Matt Parks, who led the research effort and was the original General Manager for Victory, said, "The [research] consultants in June of '93 said, 'You've got to call this [project] something so when we're faxing things to each other we don't say 'in reference to motorcycles . . . ." They said, 'Just come up with a name,' so I came up with the name 'Victory,' the Victory project."

Parks, a lifelong motorcycle enthusiast, said creating a motorcycle "has obviously been a dream of mine," and he had long thought Victory would be a good name for a motorcycle.

"Victory came along because it was a nonsensical name with positive connotations," Parks said. "It's a great name, and obviously it stuck. It's 'V for victory,' it's nostalgic, it has World War II connotations. It's as appropriate as 'Polaris' is for snowmobiles, really."

The first Victory model was named the V92C for its V-twin engine (V), engine displacement of 92 cubic inches (92), and the fact it was a cruiser (C).

"Our main goal right now is to build the brand [name recognition], so instead of calling this model the 'Rapture' or the 'Blackbird,' or whatever it might be, we're calling it the Victory V92C," Parks said. "We wanted some 'alphabet soup' so it would have a model name, but to build the brand recognition, the main focus is on the Victory name.

"When somebody says, 'What kind of bike do you have?' we want the answer to be, 'I have a Victory.'"

The research confirmed a particularly striking buying habit among cruiser owners: after purchasing a new bike, a high percentage of cruiser buyers, especially Harley-Davidson customers, immediately replaced either a few or even several components on their brand-new motorcycles. The Polaris research showed that cruisers had tremendous appeal—due in great part to the image they bestow upon riders—even though their performance or component quality was sometimes sub-par. Riders upgraded things such as brakes and intake systems for better performance, changed seats for greater comfort, and installed aftermarket exhausts for a more aggressive, more throaty exhaust note.

Parks said the research showed "there was some opportunity, it appeared, to do a better job, based on what customers were telling us and based on what the aftermarket said. We found it very interesting that, aside from the cosmetic features in the cruiser business, why are so many people changing the functional attributes of their current motorcycle?

Many of them [make changes] right away [to new bikes]. Why are they changing the wheels, the brakes, and the tires, and stiffening the frames, and adding vibration-absorption devices that you don't even see? Why are they putting on aftermarket suspensions? Some of it is obviously cosmetic, but a lot of it was functional. We needed to understand that."

Perhaps Polaris *could* make a better cruiser, but did it make business sense? Remember, shareholders were used to successful new product ventures—*and* receiving quarterly dividends.

"At that point [August 1993] we got the OK from our officer group to continue with the study," Parks said. "We all agreed that there is an opportunity in the street motorcycle business and in cruisers. We needed to determine if it fit into our manufacturing systems, and whether we could make any money at it."

Nygaard said the Victory research team recognized the risks of entering the cruiser market, especially considering the profitable popularity of

Victory fuel tanks carried this colorful tank badge from 1998–2008. For the 10th anniversary, the 2009 cruisers had a monochrome version of this logo, which Victory marketers said would be used for the next 10 years—it was used for just one year. Variations of Victory branding on bikes were first seen on 2008 Ness models, and then in high production numbers starting with the High-Ball. For 2013, Victory ditched the oval completely (it was ruled "off-brand" and was never used again) and introduced the "V"-and-bar logo. This "new" logo originally included "USA," which was later removed from tank badges to avoid the issue of whether the company claimed the bikes were American-made. (They were assembled domestically, but included globally sourced components, and vehicle manufacturers are held to strict FTC standards to legally claim "Made in the USA.") *Lee Klancher*

the Harley-Davidson culture and the "Harley rider" image and style.

"My biggest concern was: Let me sell against price, let me sell against features and benefits, let me sell against more advertising, and I can find ways to do that," Nygaard said. "Help me to sell against the lifestyle, with loyalty that is as passionate as I've ever seen on any product, i.e., Harley-Davidson. To sell against an image is very, very difficult, and that was my biggest concern."

Make Those Parts or Buy Them?

The Polaris team expected that the answer would be "Yes," they *could* make money in the motorcycle business, but they needed to determine what it would cost to build a cruiser. They did a "make versus buy" evaluation to determine which components they could produce in-house and which they would likely buy from outside vendors. In 1993, they bought a

Honda and a Harley-Davidson, disassembled them completely, estimated the cost of every single part, and determined for each part whether they would make it or buy it.

They factored in the suggested retail prices of the Honda and Harley, the dealer costs of the bikes, and the profit margin that would be required at various sales volumes.

"We came back and we felt 'Wow, there's good opportunity in this business!' So we were excited from that standpoint," Parks said. "The motorcycle would, as it turned out, fit very nicely into our existing systems, whether we built the bike in Roseau [Minnesota, site of the largest Polaris factory] or wherever else."

But what about the engine? Polaris market studies had shown that for greatest acceptance and sales appeal, a cruiser *must* have an American-made engine. (Recall Nygaard's comment about the diminished acceptance of Japanese-made—that is, *not* American-made—bikes.)

At the time, Polaris hadn't yet launched its domestic engine program, but they didn't think finding a U.S. engine supplier would be a significant stumbling block.

"Our assumption," Parks said, "was [that] we can build this engine inside [Polaris], or at least have it built in the U.S.A."

In February 1994, Parks and then-manager of manufacturing (at the company's Roseau facility) Jeff Bjorkman presented the cost findings to the company's officers.

"We got the OK from the officer group to go to prototype," Parks said. He was happy with the decision, but wondered who would do the work. Parks had no official motorcycle-related title, and more important, he had no staff.

In the summer of 1994, he and Chuck Baxter, then-vice president of engineering and product safety, hired some engineers for preliminary chassis and transmission work, "but that was really a waste of time," Parks said. "We got some work done, and we did have some competitive bikes [in hand for evaluation], so we did learn something, but until Geoff Burgess came on board in September of '94, we didn't get very much accomplished."

Burgess was the third person hired for the Victory project. Considering his leadership and his significant contributions to the project, he has to rank as one of the most significant Victory team members of all time.

Benchmarks and Goals

The Victory V92C hardly resembled a Ford Taurus, but these two disparate vehicles shared some developmental history.

Both were developed following detailed "benchmarking"—the evaluation of other vehicles to judge which had the best performance characteristics and features. With such ratings in hand, the designers and engineers (of both the Taurus and the Victory motorcycle) developed vehicles with the best-possible combinations of features at the desired price points.

In a way, it was like creating a "greatest hits" package of multiple features in a single vehicle—so long as it could be sold at the targeted suggested retail price. Victory officials felt if they achieved that goal, they would have a winner. That's what Ford achieved in the long-successful Taurus (which was developed after extensive benchmarking), and what the Victory team strived for with its own benchmarking.

"We really spent a lot of time riding the other bikes, understanding their pros and cons and trying to build something that was better," Matt Parks said. "We never tried to copy anybody. We wanted to build something that was better, that had a unique Victory flare, so at the end of the day when a guy says, 'Why do I buy a Victory motorcycle?' we can say, 'How long do you have? We'll tell you.' Or he can ride it and in five minutes, he'll know why."

Benchmarking and Data Collection

In 1994, Victory team members purchased a fleet of motorcycles—including cruisers, touring bikes, and sport bikes such as a Ducati—and evaluated every detail of each bike. These competitive bikes were ridden in Minnesota, Tennessee, and extensively in Arizona by Victory team members and Polaris engineering staffers on group benchmarking trips.

During the Arizona trip, each rider completed a three-page evaluation form during and after his ride on one of the seven competitive bikes under review. The form elicited ratings of all the performance characteristics, ergonomics, and features of each bike. Following the trip, the ratings were compiled to determine a consensus on the best version of each feature within a class (or market segment) of bike, and the best version of each feature overall.

The Victory team also assessed the cost of producing the best features to determine whether they could combine those features into a single bike and price it within the targeted Victory price range.

These steps were all part of a wide-ranging data-accumulation process that gave the Victory team a clear vision of what they wanted their motorcycle to consist of and whether such goals were fiscally possible. Among the other data collection methods were:

- As noted earlier, before the Victory project was given the green light, engineers disassembled a Honda and a Harley-Davidson and did a cost analysis of every component.

Designing the Victory began after thousands of hours of testing and evaluation, a process known as benchmarking. During 1993 and 1994, the Victory team began the process by thoroughly evaluating competitors' motorcycles. In addition to evaluating ride and performance, the Victory team disassembled two of the bikes—a 1992 Honda Shadow and a Harley-Davidson FXRS—to weigh and measure nearly every part and component group. *Lee Klancher*

• Prior to the Arizona benchmarking trip, the Victory team approached Dunlop, the tire manufacturer (and a supplier of Polaris ATV tires), to request information about motorcycle tires. With the help of Steve Paulos, a Dunlop test technician with an impressive motorcycle industry background, the Victory team gathered information about competitive motorcycles. Paulos and some of his industry contacts helped the Victory leaders learn more about competitors' development and production processes—while maintaining the level of confidentiality necessary for the Victory project to remain under wraps. Dunlop permitted Paulos to accompany the Victory team on its major Arizona benchmarking trip, and he

The Victory group's early vision for the bike, the data gathered from benchmarking, and the market demands all finally jelled into firm goals. Once this occurred, the Milwaukee-based Brooks Stevens design group was called on to put the team's vision to paper. The hidden fuel system and rear suspension as seen in this March 1995 drawing survived, though the tank-top instruments, SuperTrapp-style dual-side exhaust, and upside-down forks were scrapped. *Victory*

This Brooks Stevens drawing, also dated March 1995, shows a chunkier, taller machine. The Fat Bob tank, tank-top instrumentation, staggered duals, and crossover tube are retro cruiser, while the scalloped headlight and flared fenders offer a wink and a nod to the 1940s. *Victory*

provided valuable insights about the evaluation bikes. (He later was hired for the Victory team and subsequently became an independent consultant to the Victory project.)

- Following the Arizona benchmarking rides, the Victory team disassembled the competitive bikes and weighed and evaluated all of their components. This helped them set a target weight for the Victory bike and evaluate component materials and the production processes.

Lessons from the Desert Heat

After the benchmarking data was distilled and analyzed, the Victory team came up with goals for the bike's makeup. Among the details was the Victory engine's displacement. The Vulcan (which then had a 1,470cc engine) received the highest marks among cruiser engines on the benchmarking rides; its smoothness, acceleration, torque, and throttle response received high ratings. The Victory team determined it should take things a step further and build an even

By May 24, 1995, Brooks Stevens had turned the input of the Victory group into a close approximation of the V92C. Aggressive lines complement the stout V-twin, while subtle fender flares accentuate the elemental design. *Victory*

bigger engine to produce even more power. They settled on a displacement of 1,507cc (slightly more than 92 cubic inches). Also worth considering, of course,

To evaluate a range of chassis dimensions, the Victory group built this adjustable prototype called "Francis" in May 1995. Although it was a highly effective tool, the bike's rough appearance raised some eyebrows. "People thought it was a production model," Geoff Burgess said with a laugh. *Lee Klancher*

were the bragging rights to be gained from having the biggest cruiser engine on the market.

The Southwestern benchmarking trip also contained hard lessons that led Victory to use complementary oil cooling for its engine.

"We were stuck in this horrible Phoenix traffic, trying to get across town because none of us really knew where we were going," Parks said. "It was hotter than hell, ninety-five [degrees] in the shade and probably one-hundred-five-plus on the road. Actually, it was one of the better tests we did because we had several bikes that were liquid-cooled, some that were oil-cooled, and several that were air-cooled. On the air-cooled bikes, the cylinders appeared to, for lack of a better word, 'go square' and these brand-new bikes were just billowing smoke. I mean, *billowing* smoke! The fans would go on in the liquid-cooled bikes and they would keep nice and cool; the heat didn't do anything bad to them. They just sat there and idled in traffic.

"Interestingly enough, with the two oil-cooled bikes, one of them just acted like it did at any time,

and with the other one, the idle went up slightly. But other than that, they behaved themselves quite nicely."

Getting a Feel for the Handling

The Arizona trip also greatly helped the Victory team define its handling goals.

According to Parks, after Geoff Burgess rode one cruiser, "he said, 'I think that frame just wound up like a spring, and for every action, there's an opposite reaction.' It had to let go, and sometimes right when you were deep in the corner, it would kind of release. It was very disconcerting, and we didn't like it."

When such a chassis "uncoiled" in a turn, it gave the rider the unpleasant feeling of fighting the bike rather than riding it, particularly at higher speeds. These bikes typically had rubber-mounted engines and flexible frames, as opposed to the stiffer, more-taut chassis of the sport bikes that were evaluated.

If the Victory team were content to make a cruiser copycat that sold because of its American-made heritage and sharp styling, then sloppy handling and

During the early part of 1996, the Victory computer model became increasingly intricate. With the exterior details and dimensions nearly complete, the engineers sent their CAD (computer-aided design) files to Brooks Stevens, who generated this three-dimensional illustration in the spring of 1996. The V92C was taking shape. *Victory*

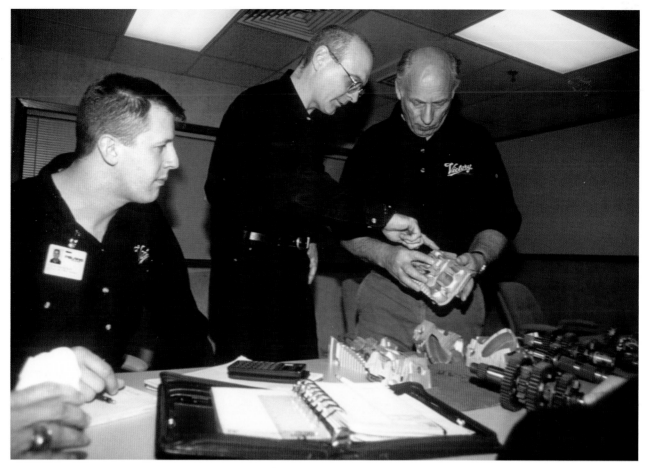

Geoff Burgess, shown conferring with Mark Bader (center) and Steve Weinzerl (seated), had been building motorcycles for more than 30 years. Experience with Triumph, Norton, and Can-Am, plus natural instincts for what motorcyclists want, and a frank, open demeanor made Burgess an ideal choice to lead Victory's engineering team. *Lee Klancher*

a soft, flexible chassis would have been acceptable. But they had set their goals much higher. They wanted to create a cruiser a rider could really push, instead of simply settling in for the ride. They wanted to build a bike that delivered a high-performance ride instead of making riders accept passive, low-speed cornering. The Victory team didn't want riders to have to back off the throttle in tight turns. They wanted the thrill of motorcycling to come from the bike's performance, not from tank badges and branded clothing.

Need proof that excellent handling was the team's top priority? Consider: the chassis and frame were designed as desired, *then* the engine was reconfigured to fit in the available space in the frame. (Details of this appear in chapter 3.)

After the Victory team determined which benchmarked bikes delivered the desired, crisp-handling ride, they did a thorough analysis of all the competitive bikes' chassis. The suspensions were

dissected and the chassis were tested for torsional rigidity.

"We measured the stiffness of each bike's chassis," said Burgess. "We compared the stiffness to the feel of the bike's handling. We chose the best [-handling chassis] and designed our chassis to match its [stiffness] number."

The approach was successful: "The first chassis we built essentially handled the way we wanted," Burgess said.

Benchmark riders' subjective ride impressions were interpreted alongside the hard data acquired from stiffness testing.

"We tried to correlate what the seat of our pants had told us first with some of the data acquisition," Parks said. "Once we'd get some actual [stiffness] numbers, we'd say 'okay, we did a torsional stiffness test of this frame and it was really a flexible frame and that's what we thought when we rode the bike.'

Geoff Burgess

When Geoff Burgess joined Victory, his impressive motorcycling background was like a brand-name-dropping feast that could have made him popular as a speaker at vintage motorcycle meets and shows around the world. But his job was to develop motorcycles for the future, not linger amid memories of yesteryear.

Turn back the clock to the mid-'60s. Scotsman Burgess worked for the Norton-Villiers Engine Company for about five years, then worked in the Triumph research center (part of the Norton Villiers Triumph Group, which later included BSA as well). There he met Mike Mills. Like Burgess, Mills would become a key player in the Victory story, but more on him later.

In 1971, the British motorcycle industry, reeling from Japanese manufacturers' rise to market dominance, collapsed. Burgess emigrated to North America while Mills struck out on his own as a consultant.

Burgess became product development engineer for Monark, a California-based motorcycle importer, and in 1976, he joined Bombardier for a 12-year run that included a stint as director of research and development for Can-Am motorcycles. He eventually went to work for Bombardier's Ski-Doo snowmobile division, but not before once again crossing paths with Mills, who worked in the 1980s for Armstrong, a European motorcycle manufacturer. (You see, from 1982 on, Can-Am motorcycles were actually Armstrong bikes with Can-Am logos.)

After leaving Bombardier, Burgess was an industrial consultant in Montreal, and he sent his résumé to Polaris. The company contracted him to assist in developing a personal watercraft prototype, but he was with Polaris only a month before a no-compete clause with his previous employer was deemed a liability.

He worked on four-wheelers—automobiles— with the GM/Delco Advanced Chassis Group in Warren, Michigan, and in 1992, just as GM offered him a position at its tech center in Paris, Polaris called. The no-compete period had elapsed, and Polaris had a job to offer.

"As I was about to take the GM job in Paris, [Polaris Engineering Vice President] Chuck Baxter called to offer me the job as head of the watercraft project," Burgess recalled. "Whatever my interest might have been, it didn't really matter, because when my wife was faced with choosing between Roseau, Minnesota, and Paris, France, you know where I ended up."

Oui.

He essentially disappeared in Europe; when Baxter sought him out in 1993 for the Victory project, none of Burgess's old U.S. contacts knew how to reach him. The fruitless search lasted several months.

"I came back to the Milford Proving Grounds in March 1994 and Jeff Smith [an old Rotax cohort] said, 'Where have you been? Polaris has been looking for you.'"

In September 1994, Burgess joined the Victory team, but only after reaching an understanding with Baxter about how the motorcycle project would proceed. Burgess had helped develop numerous vehicles, using both old and new technologies, and he wanted it understood that the project could not be rushed. He believed that thorough analysis and design work were necessary before prototypes were built; he insisted on taking this approach rather than building too-crude mules and trying to shape them into thoroughbreds.

He earned the utmost respect of Victory team members. At the outset, he sparked progress on the bike's development. As he developed a staff of engineers and designers, he offered direction, input, and freedom, entrusting them with broad responsibility to develop the best motorcycle possible. He was viewed by the staff as a manager and teacher.

"When Geoff came on board, that's when the work really started going and we laid out the whole plan for the bike," said Matt Parks. "Geoff and I worked really hard to define what the motorcycle should be. We had a general idea written up, a marketing plan, and early on Geoff had read that. But he and I had a lot of long, sit-down discussions about what the motorcycle should be. We got along real well and we agreed, pretty much from the start, what it should be. But Geoff is the consummate engineer and he wanted to do a better job and he really pushed us to do a better job."

"We realized we wanted a stiff chassis. We wanted a bike that felt like a twin, had a nice low center of gravity, but didn't vibrate so bad that your hands would go numb, your feet would go numb, and parts would fall off the bike."

The team also measured and evaluated the bikes' steering geometries. There was considerable variation in the steering angles and rake and trail measurements. This data was analyzed in relation to rider evaluations of bike handling, and revealed target geometries—those expected to deliver the desired Victory handling—which would later be applied to the first test vehicle. (See chapter 2.)

The chassis and frame analysis work was typical of the Victory team's approach to major aspects of the bike; they did extensive analysis before ever building prototypes so the prototypes would be as refined as possible from the outset. This resulted in highly efficient and effective development work on the prototypes. It also took advantage of the

The first prototypes with Victory engines are shown as C bikes. Although most of these were very roughly finished, the bike shown was painted and finished for a presentation to the board of directors. The engine fins were polished with a belt sander, handmade aluminum pieces hide the bolt holes for the rear seat mount, and the Victory script on the handlebar mount was laser-printed on an overhead transparency sheet, cut out, and glued on. *Victory*

capabilities of state-of-the-art design and analysis software.

"It was design by mathematics, not by iteration," Burgess said. "Some people weren't comfortable with it. They wanted to see some prototypes, wanted to see us build something, but we took our time and did it right before building anything."

The entire project "[has] been a fairly rapid development cycle but a lot of up-front thinking has saved us a lot of time on the back end," Parks said.

Once they had collected and analyzed loads of chassis data, they met "Francis."

Learning Lessons from 'Francis'

A rolling prototype used in the development of a vehicle, whether it's a car, truck, motorcycle, or ATV, is commonly called a mule. It's typically a working beast that's long on function and short on styling. It might not be pretty, but it will work long hours, take loads of abuse, and ideally, teach the development technicians a lot about the vehicle they're creating.

Such was the case with "Francis," the mule used to develop the Victory chassis. (This two-wheeled beast was named after Francis the Talking Mule,

The next generation of development bikes was the PD bikes. The major difference between the C and PD bikes was a redesigned frame. This is PD-2, perhaps the only PD bike to use the older C frame. *Lee Klancher*

It ain't pretty, but critical chassis development was done with this battered beast. Built in May 1995, with a right-hand belt drive V-twin engine and adjustable chassis, Francis the Mule was used to determine optimum chassis dimensions. The mule's wheels, Fox shocks, and Marzocchi forks carried over to later prototypes, while the rubber-mounted engine was changed to a solid-mounted powerplant for superior torsional stiffness. *Lee Klancher*

the four-legged star of six silly but popular movies produced between 1949 and 1956.)

Antoine Pharamond, a young project engineer straight out of the California aircraft industry, started designing Francis in early 1995 so the Victory team could develop a chassis that offered the responsive handling the team demanded. Francis was the road-going step beyond the computer design and analysis work that had already done on the chassis. The mule let the team: determine the steering geometry needed to deliver the responsive handling they wanted; learn whether the frame and chassis would meet their torsional stiffness goals; and refine the suspensions.

Matt Parks said, "The bike was starting to take form on paper. We agreed, 'It should weigh about this much, it should have this, it should have that.' At that point, we started building a mule, which basically meant taking the geometry that we had laid out and building this adjustable chassis to learn

absolutely as much as we could about the geometry, the seating position, and the ergonomics to make this thing, from a chassis standpoint, be better than cruisers currently on the market."

Francis is Born

Pharamond, Victory technician Jere Peterson, Steve Paulos (originally in charge of Victory testing and development), Parks, and Geoff Burgess developed the mule in a creative, efficient fashion: The chassis was adjustable. The frame was built with the torsional rigidity the team wanted (based on benchmarking), and selected components could be mounted in varied positions.

"The mule had the desired stiffness built into it, but we could adjust the geometry," Paulos said. "We could change the steering head angle and change the trail and rake, among other things. By only changing one thing at a time we could really evaluate changes."

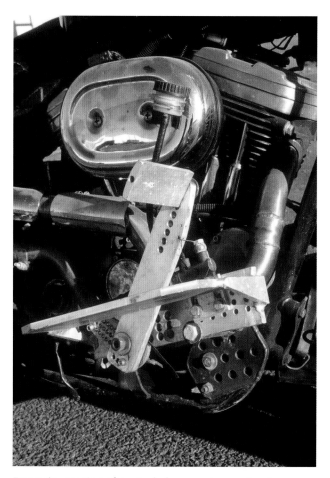

By adjusting the mule's crucial chassis dimensions—wheelbase, steering-head angle, rake, trail, swingarm pivot location, and more—the victory team was able to test major design changes with the twist of a couple bolts. *Lee Klancher*

Extensive testing of control placement was also done with the mule. Load cells were mounted on the levers to gather data, while test riders did the same. The results were compared to the data gathered during benchmarking and used to determine leverage ratios and placement that gave the best feel and action. *Lee Klancher*

The swingarm pivot location was adjustable and the bike's center of gravity could also be altered.

Paulos had previously done developmental work for Honda on the six-cylinder Gold Wing and Pacific Coast models. During such projects, test chassis had not been adjustable, so making chassis geometry changes was much more complicated and time-consuming than it was with Francis.

On prior projects, Paulos said, "you had to cut things apart, and when you welded them back together, you weren't sure you weren't changing something else along with what you wanted to adjust."

Francis's primary task was to help the team achieve its distinct goals for the Victory ride and handling.

"This bike was being designed to really go around a corner because, obviously, people on the team wanted

to give their input into the design, and these guys like to ride at a fairly decent pace," Parks said. "I mean, they're not road-racing a cruiser, but they wanted this bike to have real good handling characteristics."

Parks and Burgess compared cruisers of the '90s to big, soft-handling luxury cars of another era.

"Geoff and I felt a lot of the cruisers looked good and they felt good and all that, but their handling was kind of like a mid-'70s luxury car, they kind of had marshmallow handling," Parks said. "You wouldn't want to go around the corner *too* fast on this bike, but look where those same [luxury] cars are today—Cadillacs, Lincolns, BMWs, Mercedes, and Lexus: They're fast, have good brakes, and they go around a corner really well. They're very much sportier than they were in the '70s, and we took the same approach: 'Why *can't* a cruiser go in that direction? Why shouldn't it handle really well?' It would help differentiate us, also."

Paulos knew from prior career experience that a big bike could be designed to handle easily. Once the V92C reached market, he looked back and said the Victory team succeeded in reaching its handling goals.

"What we were looking for was something with a light and nimble feel even though it's a six-hundred-pound motorcycle," he said. "I had been so impressed at Honda by how easily the GL1500 [Gold Wing] handled even though it was an eight-hundred-pound bike. With the Victory, we developed a confidence-inspiring motorcycle. It doesn't do anything to scare you. As we developed the chassis, I was thinking about the customer, and they're not all experienced. I wanted to make it a ride they'd be comfortable with, enjoy, and feel safe."

But that ride was achieved only after Francis rolled up thousands of miles and the team—and others—logged countless hours in the office and shop.

Although the Victory team worked independently (not sharing staff with other Polaris product divisions), they received valuable input from some Polaris engineers.

"The mule was getting really well-defined and we had some early drawings of the frame, but we were sort of struggling with some frame components, and we got some excellent help from people like Mihai," Parks said of Mihai Rasidescu, then a Polaris ATV engineer. Chassis development was also aided by at least two other Polaris engineering staffers: Glen Arneson, a CAD designer, and Guoguang Chen, who provided valuable Finite Element Analysis (FEA) assistance. (The FEA process uses complex computer software to analyze designs and structure to determine stress and load paths in components such as frames. Using FEA software, the Victory team learned where the greatest stresses would be on the frame and chassis components, allowing them to make structural adjustments.)

Mario Negri, a 1995 summer intern, was hired in the summer of 1996 as a design engineer. He had a flair for styling and aesthetic design: He took the sound fundamental work of Rasidescu, Arneson,

By using an existing engine to power the mule, Victory engineers were able to develop an ideal chassis before they committed to the engine design. This slave engine was chosen because the dimensions, integral gearbox, and right-side output shaft matched what was planned for the V92C powerplant. As a result of what was learned from the mule, the specified length for the Victory engine was shortened more than 15 percent. *Lee Klancher*

Chen, et al., and added some design style to the frame and swingarm. Using Chen's FEA findings, Negri was able to reduce the weight of the frame by 20 pounds by the time it was ready for production.

The Makeup of the Mule

There were two significant reasons why Francis was solely a test bed for chassis makeup and handling, not for Victory engine development: First, chassis

Steve Paulos oversaw much of the chassis development done with the mule. Paulos's experience developing the Honda Gold Wing and Pacific Coast was key to the Victory's agile, forgiving handling. Paulos is shown in the original Victory shop in Osceola, Wisconsin, near one of the early CV bikes. *Lee Klancher*

development was a top priority because of the team's insistence that the bike offer superb handling. Second, at the time, there was no engine design staff—Engine Design Manager Mark Bader hadn't even been hired when Francis was born. (He was hired in May 1995.)

Since no Victory test engine existed in early 1995, when Peterson was assembling Francis, a "slave" engine was needed. Because it had a right-hand-side belt drive, as the V92C would have, a Harley-Davidson Sportster 1200 engine was installed in the mule.

"The engine was solidly mounted, and there was a horrible vibration," said Burgess. "There was great frame flex, and the high-speed stability was not great, but it wasn't expected to be because the frame had bolts everywhere, like Frankenstein."

(At the time, plans still called for the Victory engine to be rubber-mounted, not solid-mounted to the frame. Thus, the mule wasn't designed to accommodate a solid-mounted engine, and the significant vibration was not a primary concern.)

In contrast to the engine, the mule's suspension components were very similar to eventual production parts.

"We had our own custom forks, the production forks, so we started to play around with the spring rates and the damping rates on Francis, and then we did the same thing with the rear shock using a Fox shock, which is basically what we're using now, just modified," Burgess said.

The mule's Marzocchi forks had big—for a cruiser—45mm tubes. By comparison, most cruisers at the time had forks in the 36mm to 42mm range. The Victory team sought the larger forks to ensure the chassis would have the desired rigidity, and, in a marketing move, to earn bragging rights for having

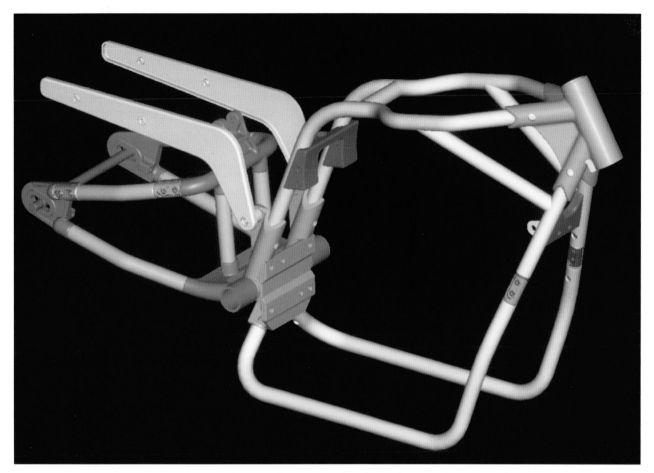

The testing that Paulos and others did with the mule was translated into the ideal dimensions for the frame. This computer-generated image shows a preproduction version of the frame used on the C bikes and at least one of the PD bikes. The cross-pieces near the steering head are the major giveaway that this is an early frame. *Victory*

the biggest forks on the market—at least for the time being.

"The torsional rigidity of the forks is better when you go with the bigger size, so there is an advantage," Burgess said. "Plus, we did a survey, collected the [competitors' measurements], and said, 'We want to be bigger than what's out there because either by the time we're out there, everybody will be at that level, or we'll have an advantage. They're getting bigger and bigger on the market.'"

Why Marzocchi forks? They were selected because they were outstanding products, because a North American supplier couldn't be found, and because there wasn't a Japanese vendor capable of giving the Victory team the engineering input it sought along with the hard parts.

Burgess recalled: "With my previous connections with Marzocchi from Bombardier, where we had used them in Can-Ams, we talked to Marzocchi and they said, 'Oh, yeah, we've got forty-five-millimeter Magnum forks. We've won seventeen World Championships with these forks, and we can build you a street version of them.' That's how we ended up with our forty-fives."

The Victory engineering team got assistance and feedback from Marzocchi's technicians, but the aluminum fork slider was an original Victory concept, as was the design of the triple clamps. These were designed by Lewis Vaughn, an Arizona transplant to Minnesota.

To evaluate existing steering geometries and set target angles for the Victory, the team benchmarked the competition, measuring the rake and trail of numerous bikes, primarily cruisers.

"We looked at a spectrum of the market, a Kawasaki Vulcan, a [Harley-Davidson] Road King

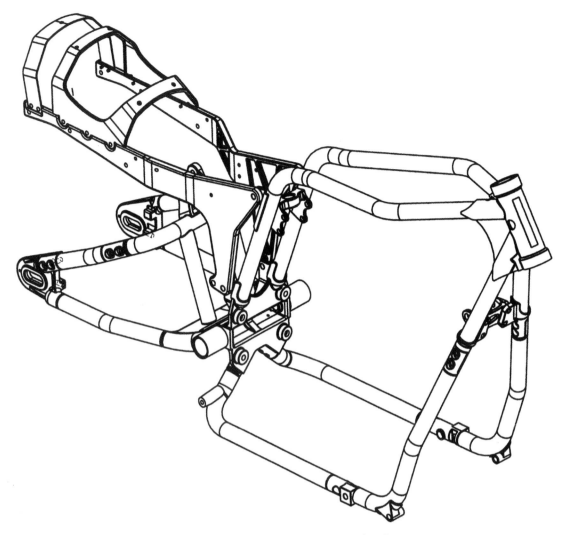

Once the dimensions of the frame were determined, finite element analysis (FEA) was used to identify key stress points. This allowed the frame to shed about 20 pounds and yet maintain the rigidity required by the Victory team's parameters. The lightened frame was used on most of the Victory preproduction bikes. *Victory*

Softail, a Yamaha Virago, probably six different models," Burgess said. "We plotted their rakes and trails on a graph so we had a scatter plot of these points and saw that, 'Wow, these guys are all over the place,' from thirty-two degrees rake to twenty-eight degrees rake, with different trails as well."

The team analyzed how the numbers for these bikes compared to one another, taking into consideration how each one's handling had been rated during benchmarking rides. They then settled on targets of 30 degrees rake and five inches of trail.

"That's what we found to be the best compromise without too much sacrifice either way," Burgess said.

Why this talk of compromise and sacrifice?

It was because the team was actually developing a chassis for two, and perhaps more, different

bikes. In the long-range Victory plan, the standard cruiser, the V92C, would be followed onto the market by other cruiser models. That second Victory model was expected to have a higher-performance version of the 92-cubic-inch engine, sportier handling than the original Victory model, and different forks.

To maximize efficiency in all areas—from engineering and design to purchasing and assembly—the team wanted to make the original Victory chassis adaptable for the second cruiser. They set out to develop a chassis that would initially deliver the desired V92C ride and, with minor modifications, would work in the second cruiser chassis. *That* was the compromise they wanted to keep to a minimum, and they believed they had succeeded.

The Victory frame is a three-piece unit that uses the engine as a stressed member. The backbone of the frame wraps around the top of the engine, providing a main beam of support somewhat similar to the twin aluminum spars used on current sportbikes. The other two pieces wrap around the bottom left and right of the engine. *Lee Klancher*

Through testing, the team determined chassis geometry for the V92C model, then developed a second setup for the second cruiser by changing the rake, trail, and wheelbase, and using different wheels and tires. They found the median between the two setups "and we did another check on that to see if we could get the two cruisers to have a common geometry," Burgess said. "We found out we could get

enough differentiation between those two models by the suspension and tires and other changes that we'd have between the two, still using the same [chassis] geometries."

In fact, Burgess felt that having a chassis with the strengths of each model—the standard cruiser's stiffness and the second cruiser's steering geometry—would make both models better.

"What we've ended up with is a more sporty standard cruiser, and because we have this thick chassis, engine, and forks, I think we're going to end up with a better second cruiser as well."

The V92C had 5¼ inches of front suspension travel, more than most cruisers, but that figure included an allowance for sag-in (the amount the forks compress when a rider sits on the bike), so the usable travel was actually about 4¼ inches.

A Legend's Impact on the Rear Suspension

Some elements of the V92C design were dictated by marketing. After all, despite being unique, the bike had to also have traits that were popular with, and familiar to, cruiser enthusiasts. According to Burgess, one such marketing directive concerned the rear suspension.

"Marketing dictated that we have a traditional triangular swingarm without any rear shocks on the outside. We didn't want twin shocks on the sides."

Familiar with vintage British motorcycles, Burgess suggested a swingarm and suspension setup that dated back to a legendary marque.

"We looked at the Vincent, which originally had a dual shock under [the seat], and eventually ended up with a single shock under there, which, basically, Yamaha copied [from Vincent]. We knew that we had to go that route because that was the only way [to get what we wanted] without linkages. We didn't want any linkages or anything with a rocker arm setup. We wanted a simple setup—that worked."

The team used its anti-squat goals to determine where to locate the swingarm pivot, and this in turn

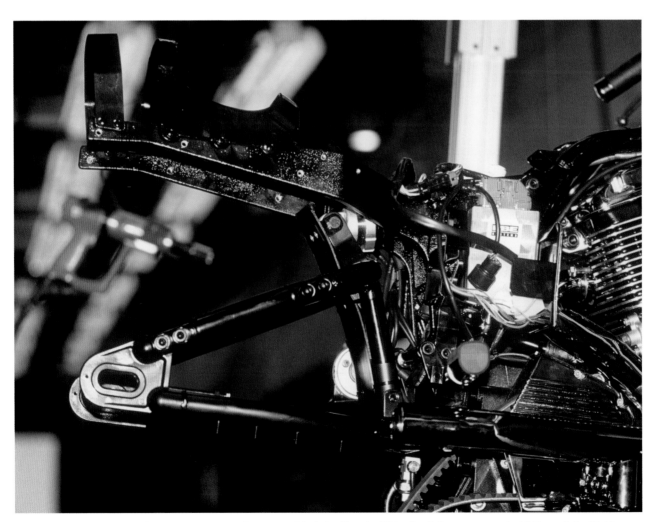

Styling dictated a triangular rear swingarm that resembled the "hardtail" look of the unsuspended bikes of the 1940s. The rider's posterior demands suspension. The simple and effective result was a single shock mounted underneath the seat, with an aluminum subframe supporting the seat and rear fender. *Lee Klancher*

Invented and marketed by Greg McDonald (left), the GMD Computrak precisely measured chassis dimensions such as rake, trail, wheel offset, and more by triangulating a number of data points on the motorcycle's wheel and frame. The Computrak unit functioned as a quality control device and was used in chassis development of future models.

Lee Klancher

helped position the final drive, the rearmost section of the driveline.

Burgess said, "We figured out where the swingarm position—and therefore the gearbox output position—needed to be to get the anti-squat number right for the power on and off, throttle on and throttle off."

The rear suspension had four inches of travel, about standard among cruisers, and the rear shock had a pre-load adjuster: a threaded collar with which a rider could increase or decrease the pre-load. Parks, for one, expected few problems with, or complaints about, the rear shock.

"It's got a Fox shock that you would have to pay hundreds of dollars for in the aftermarket to put on another cruiser," he said. "We wanted this [high-quality shock] to be a standard feature."

Extending toward the rear of the bike—unseen under the rear fender and the seats—was a strong but lightweight aluminum sub-frame.

"It has quite a lot of load subjected on it when you go through a 'G bump.' There are a lot of G forces there," Burgess explained, "so we wanted to tie the whole thing together, locate the rear fender and seats and make sure that we had some integrity. Negri designed a cast aluminum sub-frame and we bolted it on the main frame to minimize distortion so we can control where the sub-frame and everything else is going to end up."

Burgess said it was a marketing directive that the sub-frame's two main arms be covered and not exposed, so that they would be hidden by the fender and linked for strength as well.

"We had to tie the two parts together because these things just like to walk around on their own. They're like a three-foot arm waving around back there. We tied them in with a bracket and some loops in the back to make it a good structure and to be able to put the seats on there so the weight [on the seats] would be evenly distributed."

Resizing the Engine

Once the frame and chassis took shape, the engine team had to adapt the power plant to the available space.

"We eventually came up with the engine space, and they had to make the engine fit in the frame," Burgess said. "We shrank the engine to make it fit, yet all critical factors in the power-on and handling dynamics were considered in the locating of the gearbox sprocket. We had to change the engine's V angle from fifty-five degrees to fifty degrees to get the engine to fit and get the horizontal [rear] shock in place, so the cylinders' center-to-center distance grew closer."

Burgess acknowledged that the frame-first development process might be unusual, but he felt it was proper in the case of the V92C.

"It's backwards in terms of timing, but not in terms of the design process," he said. "This way, we ended up with the chassis and the way to deliver the ride and handling we want rather than letting the engine size determine the bike's size and layout. There was no ride compromise in this process."

The decision to solid-mount the engine in the frame and make it a stressed member (covered in depth in chapter 4) further ensured that the chassis would retain the desired rigidity.

"The original parameter was to rubber-mount the engine," said Mark Bader, who joined the original team to work on the engine and later became design manager. "The more we looked at that, the more we decided it was a bad idea. The number one reason is because the engine is far stiffer as a unit than the chassis is, and it didn't make any sense for us to take the stiffest thing in the bike and isolate it from the frame."

Manx Magic

Geoff Burgess's British motorcycle heritage paid off more than once as the Victory chassis was developed, including the time he encouraged then-engine design manager Mark Bader to lower the crankshaft. The Victory team was close to achieving its desired chassis design and handling, but something was not quite right. Burgess dusted off a memory and it paid off. Here's his account:

"Something I knew from my days at Norton and the famous Manx Norton and its Featherbed frame—which would handle like it was on rails—was the location of the crankshaft centerline and the axle centerlines. The Manx Norton had a magic about it, and if you took a Featherbed frame and put another engine in there, it didn't handle the same.

"The magic was supposed to be that if you had all three gyroscopes in line, it worked. So, in other words, the center of the front wheel, the center of the crankshaft, and the center of the rear wheel were in line, and this was supposed to be some sort of a miracle magic. I told Mark about this and we dropped the centerline of the crankshaft one inch to accommodate that while still keeping the ground clearance. We moved the sump up a bit so we didn't compromise the ground clearance at full bump."

Bader cited that alignment as the reason the bike felt light and maneuverable in corners. "A lot of that is attributable to a low center of gravity, and that's all pushed by having that crankshaft below the [wheels'] center line. It's slightly below, it's not a lot, it's not an inch below, it's a couple millimeters below, but it is below that center line and it makes a huge difference in how the bike feels."

In Search of Bad Roads

Geoff Burgess had what seemed like a strange way of making friends in a new town. But then, he was trying to develop motorcycles, not gather tourism information.

"A good guy to always drop in on is the county road engineer," Burgess said, "and that's what we did in Tennessee [where the mule was tested]. We dropped in on this guy and asked, 'Where are the shittiest roads that you've got?' The stock answer is 'What? We get guys *complaining* about the shitty roads, not asking for them.'"

Burgess followed the same routine in Polk County, Wisconsin, where Osceola, home to the Victory engineering center, is located. The county highway engineer was an old motorcycle enthusiast who had heard rumors of the Victory project and offered to help anytime he could.

He eventually lent a hand when the Victory team needed a precision pothole for some suspension data acquisition testing.

"From my days at GM, I knew that the pothole test was the most severe thing for chassis shock loading," Burgess said. "They do a twenty-eight-mile-per-hour test over a standard pothole at the GM proving grounds. I gave [Test Engineer] Robin Tuluie the dimensions of this pothole and told him to go see this highway guy."

A highway crew was tearing up a road for repair and agreed to "fabricate" (Burgess's term) the test pothole. What were its dimensions? According to Burgess: "It's six inches deep with a ramp. You have a three-foot run-in, and then there's a ramp up to the six-inch face, so it's not quite vertical. But it bottomed the forks out completely. It worked fine for our test."

Francis the Mule was fitted with accelerometers to measure the force of the impact, and Tuluie and technician Tom Manley hit the hole at the proper test speed several times. All the while, the road crew looked on, "wondering, 'What the hell are they doing?'" Burgess said.

It was believed—correctly, it turns out—that if the engine were solid-mounted, a balance shaft would be required to rein in the vibration the engine produced.

"I said, 'Okay, I can put a balance shaft in there and we can get rid of all the primaries [vibration frequencies] and we'll just have the [less-substantial] secondaries left and we can have a much stiffer chassis,'" Bader said.

It also relieved the team of having to learn about, develop, or acquire suitable rubber engine mounts.

Burgess recalled: "The balance shaft, Mark basically drove that, saying 'we need a balance shaft, that's the only way to go, we don't want that rubber[-mounting] stuff,' because we didn't understand this rubber stuff at all. You read about how Harley-Davidson spent something like fifteen years getting it right and we had to get it right within two years. We thought, 'that's a no-brainer' [to solid-mount the engine], so we went with a balance shaft."

Lessons Learned, Challenges Faced

As they did with other aspects of the bike, the team learned a lot about suspensions and chassis design while developing the bike. They said that this on-the-job expansion of their knowledge base equipped them to capably develop future bikes and to respond to any problems that arose with production bikes.

"We spent a lot of engineering time understanding the geometry of the rear end," Parks said.

What was the biggest challenge faced in developing the entire chassis?

"I would say the linking of the frame to the engine so everything is solid, so we had a good, solid connection and everything lined up," Burgess said. "You know, the engine is built in a separate plant from the chassis, and therefore we really needed to make sure that all of the castings and brackets came within a proper tolerance, so we knew the thing would mount up solid—without a lever or crow bar!"

Developing a Big-Bore V-Twin from Scratch

In the early stages of the motorcycle project, the Victory staff determined the bike had to excel in two key performance areas: its handling and its power. Marketing studies told General Manager Matt Parks that the engine had to be a big V-twin, and it had to be U.S.-made; an American company like Polaris couldn't import the engine for a bike whose target buyers love the patriotic aspect of the cruiser culture. The timing of the Victory project was fortuitous; in the early 1990s, Polaris was considering starting its own engine manufacturing operation.

A little background: From the mid-1960s until 1995, every Polaris snowmobile and watercraft engine came from Fuji Heavy Industries, a Japanese supplier. Polaris ATV engines came from Fuji or from Robin Manufacturing, a Wisconsin-based joint venture between Polaris and Fuji.

From the time Polaris first purchased snowmobile engines from Fuji in the mid-1960s, the two companies built a long and mutually beneficial relationship.

Although the Victory group seriously considered going to outside vendors for engine design, Polaris Engine Design Manager Martin Heinrich helped convince the group it was possible to do it in-house. The 91.92-cubic inch result uses ports designed by wizard Mike Mills (who also worked on Kenny Roberts's Modenas KR3 Grand Prix race bike). With 75 rear-wheel horsepower on tap, test rider Cory McWhorter easily roasted the Victory's 160/80 Dunlop elite. *Lee Klancher*

The parameters for the Victory engine were first laid out by Geoff Burgess in November 1994. The design was massaged by Victory engineers, and in February 1995, Brooks Stevens created this concept drawing. Note the exposed pushrods, which were dropped when the decision was made to go with a single overhead cam.
Victory

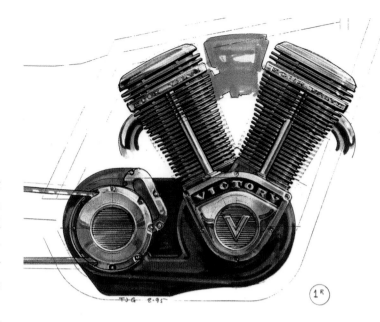

It wasn't dissatisfaction with Fuji or its product that led Polaris to consider a domestic engine project in the 1990s. Rather, it was a combination of external factors, both positive (the opportunity for total design, development, and manufacturing control over engine projects) and negative (the volatile exchange rate between U.S. and Japanese currencies).

Polaris launched its engine project with great success. The first domestically produced Polaris engines were used in 1996 watercraft and 1997 snowmobiles. Today, Polaris engines are used in the majority of the vehicles the company produces.

Once it was decided that Victory engines would be built not only in the United States but by the company itself, the company's Osceola, Wisconsin, facility—previously the site of engine assembly operations—became home to the Victory engine team in December 1995. Victory engines were produced in Osceola through the end of production (2016 for engines), with the exception of the Empulse electric motor, which came from Brammo in Oregon.

Engine Alternatives

It wasn't always certain that the Victory division would produce its own engines. In fact, Victory team members Burgess and Parks traveled to Europe in March 1995 with members of the Polaris engineering department such as Chuck Baxter, then-vice president, engineering, to evaluate potential engine suppliers.

In England, they visited: Lotus, the sports-car maker and former Formula 1 car race team; Cosworth, which produced Indy car and F1 engines for Ford; and Triumph, the motorcycle manufacturer for whom Burgess worked in its first life. (Production of "original" Triumphs ceased in 1982. The name changed hands and production of new-generation Triumphs started in 1990.) They additionally visited Ducati and Aprilia in Italy, and BMW in Germany.

"Cosworth had built a Norton engine in the '70s," Burgess said. "We wanted to look into getting engine design help from either Cosworth or Lotus. The potential bill from Cosworth was enormous, much too costly, and Lotus was very cagey. We figured out they were working on someone else's engine."

At each stop on the trip, Burgess said, "we examined the manufacturing techniques and evaluated whether they could produce what we were looking for. At that time, we were still asking, 'Who's going to design the engine and who's going to build it?'"

At Baxter's direction, the team benchmarked engines made by Fuji and Cosworth, engines from BMW and Kawasaki motorcycles, and a Dodge Neon engine for manufacturing and assembly insights.

Why did they benchmark a Neon?

"This was a new generation for Chrysler, and they had some really neat ways they drove the camshafts, they minimized the mass of the engine, and the way they mounted it," Burgess said. "It was good to look at the technologies they had. A lot of it wasn't compatible with a motorcycle engine, but it showed you hey, they did something different, they thought outside the box, and it was good to look at that."

One consideration was to have Cosworth provide cylinder head design while the Victory team would do as much engine development as possible, learning what Burgess called "the technology of engine design" through contact with Cosworth and work on the first engine. The potential flaws in that approach were considerable; there was the chance that the Victory team wouldn't be able to learn all the intricacies of engine design, and by the second time around, would either still be dependent on an outside supplier, or be making mistakes that experienced designers would avoid.

"We thought that, long-term, we needed to develop an internal competency of engine design and engine development," Parks said.

Thus, the engine was approached with a hands-on, "Let's learn how to do this ourselves" approach. That gave the team first-hand design experience that enabled them to sort out potential problems and design subsequent Victory models.

Setting the Parameters

In November 1994, Geoff Burgess told Martin Heinrich and the Victory team of the original design specifications of the Victory four-stroke engine. These specs would be revised several times as the engine was discussed and designed.

According to Burgess, the original Victory V92C was projected as a 75-bhp (at 4,300 rpm) engine.

As provided by Burgess, the original, projected specifications included:

- 97mm bore, 102mm stroke, 1,507cc, bore/stroke ratio of 0.95
- V angle of 55 degrees between cylinder centerlines
- pushrod OHV, four valves per cylinder, solid lifters
- exhaust pipe exits to be on same side
- balance factor TBD [to be determined] in chassis, no balancer, engine to be rubber-mounted in frame . . .
- air-cooled
- fuel supply by carb
- two engine mounting points, swingarm and front

Burgess recalled: "We also assessed the risk factor—the potential of achieving the engine goals versus the

In May 1995, engine designer Mark Bader came onboard to turn parameters into horsepower. While Bader began designing the engine on the computer screen, consultant Mike Mills was enlisted to ensure the powerplant not only made ample horsepower, but also had the potential for more. *Lee Klancher*

schedule and under cost—and 'missing technologies.' That is, were the required manufacturing processes available to us in the industry." (That first engine memo, from which the projected specifications cited above were drawn, rated the risk factor as "low" and the missing technologies as "none.")

The Victory engine specifications changed, of course, but the team didn't make a complete U-turn; they simply changed course in some areas. For example: pushrods were never used, the exhaust outlets were positioned front and rear, and the engine was fuel-injected, oil-cooled, solid-mounted, and had a balance shaft.)

Engine Design Gets Rolling

Engine development accelerated once a staff concentrating solely on the engine was assembled, starting with the May 1995 hiring of Mark Bader to head

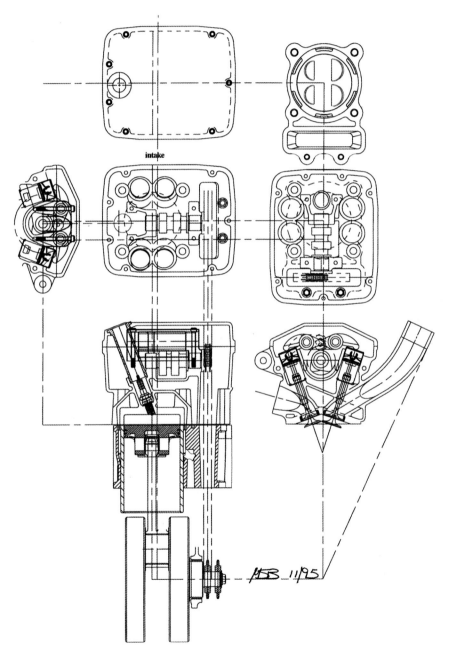

intake

Mike Mills's input was key to the Victory's substantial horsepower. Two of Mills's crucial designs are visible in this Bader drawing from November 1995. Mills drew from his high-performance experience to direct the angle and shape of the ports, vital ingredients for the high-volume flow necessary for big horsepower. Mills also proposed offset rocker arms that would move the single cam over enough to mount the spark plug centrally and close to vertical. *Lee Klancher*

up engine design. A former Kohler engine designer, Bader took the original engine parameters and began revising and refining the engine makeup. He was also charged with hiring the engine staff, which he began in June 1995 by hiring Scott Walter, a former Carrier refrigeration company designer who made valuable contributions to the Victory engine.

"Scott was an enthusiastic guy but he came from Carrier and had done heating units, but he had never designed an engine before," Bader said. "He is an extremely hard-working guy, though, and he had road-raced motorcycles and had motorcycles. It was basically just the two of us [working on the engine] until we moved to Osceola. Scott and I pounded out a tremendous amount of work in the first six months."

The engine—which originally consisted of about 340 parts—was always projected as a high-powered, big-bore V-twin, and that didn't change. The engine retained its original bore and stroke of 97×102mm, and the displacement held firm at 1,507cc (91.92 cubic inches).

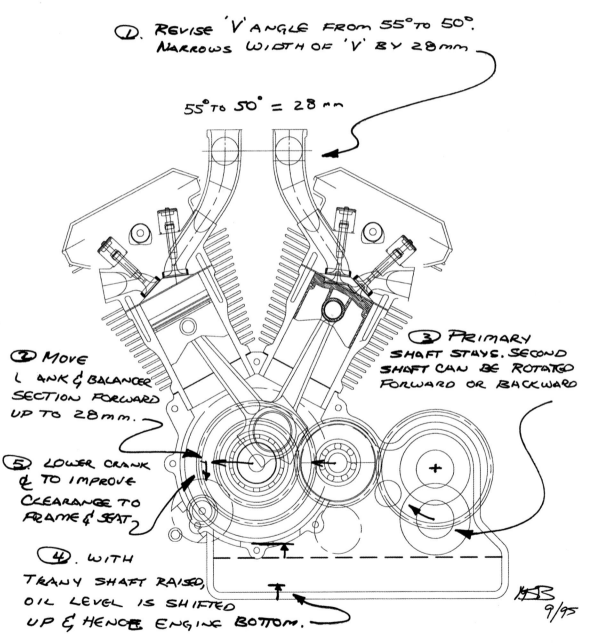

In the fall of 1995, research done with the mule demonstrated that the top of the engine needed to be narrowed by about 28mm to optimize the Victory's handling. This September 1995 engine drawing shows Bader's proposed modifications to narrow the engine. *Victory*

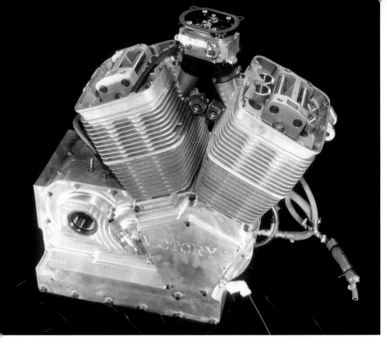

By the summer of 1996, the Victory team had the top-end parts it needed to test the engine, but was waiting for crankcases. The team decided to have heavy-duty, simplified engine cases carved from a 350-pound block of aluminum billet. The result became known as the "Hammer." *Lee Klancher*

The V angle was originally projected at 55 degrees, but as noted in chapter 3, when the frame was refined, the space for the engine was too cramped for such a wide engine, and the V was reduced to 50 degrees.

The cylinders had Nikasil-lined bores, which were effective at transferring heat away from the combustion chamber, and the oil-cooling jackets were concentrated toward the top ends of the cylinders, nearest the combustion chambers. The pistons were lightweight and had short skirts, and the connecting rods were stout and made of steel.

As noted earlier, the Arizona benchmarking trip led to the team decision to use oil as its cooling medium rather than water (or a traditional coolant-water mixture). The switch to oil cooling posed no major design problems. The six quarts of oil were used for cooling and lubrication, and were circulated by dual oil pumps driven by balance shaft gearing. The oil was exposed to cooling airflow in the frame-mounted oil cooler.

After only a few (and exhausting) minutes of cranking the engine over, the Victory team was elated when they first heard the ear-splitting roar of the unsilenced Hammer at the shop in Osceola, Wisconsin. *Victory*

Following testing in Death Valley, California, the team increased the size of the oil cooler by about 30 percent, but that was the biggest cooling system design change following the concept stage. Steve Weinzierl, the product development manager for engines, said that during follow-up testing using the larger cooler, the Victory engine achieved team cooling goals even in 100-degree-plus desert heat—while pulling a sidecar loaded with test equipment.

The oil's cooling efforts were complemented by each cylinder's 21 cooling fins. Slightly tapered and left with as-cast, unfinished surfaces (not polished smooth), the fins transferred heat and directed airflow to the cylinder body.

A couple of styling notes: The head gasket joint was barely visible amid the upper fins. This was done intentionally to give each cylinder a seamless, one-piece look. And the dipstick extending up from the crankcase on the right side of the bike was enhanced with styling, too.

'Modern' SOHC Displaces Pushrod Plan

The original concept of using rocker arms to control the valves didn't last long. The idea gave way early in

While the Hammer's cases were one-off CNC units, the heads were essentially production-tooled. The oil-cooling passages were similar to those used on water-cooled bikes. Note the offset placing of the valvetrain and the chambers where the overhead hydraulic lifters rest. *Lee Klancher*

the engine design process to a single overhead cam (SOHC) setup.

"This is a modern engine design that's going to last ten or fifteen years into the future, and push rods are not what we want," Bader said.

The engine team's challenge: design a SOHC layout without increasing the engine height. After all, the engine already filled the allotted frame space. Also, Parks said he didn't want to see external indications of an OHC setup as seen on some foreign bikes.

The engine height was preserved when the cams were sunk low in the heads, something Bader had worked on in a Kohler engine just prior to joining Polaris, so the approach was fresh in his mind.

The cams were controlled by chains driven by the crankshaft, and the chains were hidden in tunnels built into the cylinder walls on the right side of the engine. Since the cooling fins ran top-to-bottom on the cylinders, they helped mask any external sign of the tunnels. In keeping with the goal of an exceptionally low-maintenance engine, the cam chain tensioners were self-adjusting.

In each cylinder head, a cam controlled two rocker arms, and each arm had a twin-pronged roller rocker to activate two valves apiece (two intake, two exhaust),

The Hammer was built only for testing. It had no transmission or clutch. The cases were four times as thick as production units. "You could light a bomb off in those things," Bader said, "and not get hurt." *Lee Klancher*

By August 1996, an engine was installed in C-3, an early preproduction bike. The engine was a paper tiger—literally. This engine was created by entering the CAD drawings into the Victory rapid-prototyping machine, which built the mock-up using thousands of precisely cut pieces of paper glued together. Known as LOM (laminated object manufacturing) parts, these computer-generated mock-ups allowed parts to be generated and test-fit without the excessive cost of CNC parts. *Victory*

and no-maintenance hydraulic lifters. The spark plug in each head was accessible (using a standard socket) via an opening extending down through the head at an angle.

"In a perfect world, you want the spark plug pointed straight up and down," Bader said. "With a dual OHC, you can do that. With our SOHC, we had to miss the cam," so the spark plug sneaks in under the cam at an angle.

Because the engine was solid-mounted and a stressed member of the bike's chassis, standard gaskets couldn't be trusted to endure the chassis loading. Thus, laminated steel gaskets were used for the head gasket, base gasket, and valve cover gasket. The steel gaskets held up well during all forms of engine testing, and unlike traditional gaskets, weren't prone to creep or deteriorate over time.

Assembling the Hammer began on September 2, 1996. The Victory group put in a grueling string of 18-hour days over Labor Day weekend to get the first Victory engine hooked up and on the dyno. *Victory*

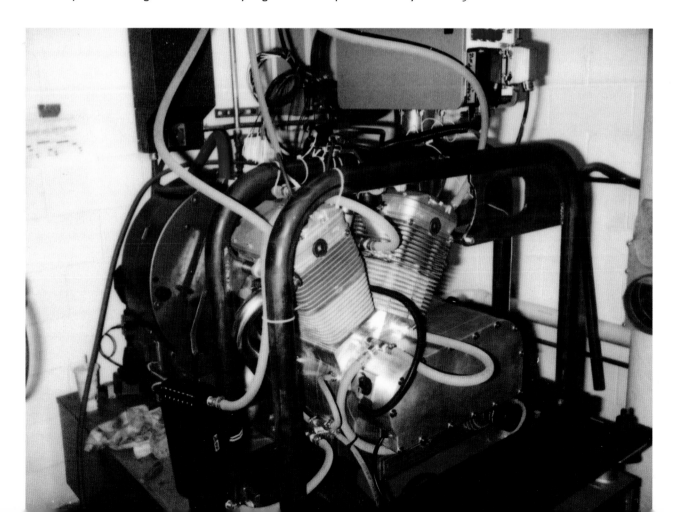

A lot of sleepless nights put the Hammer in the dyno room at Osceola, Wisconsin, on September 6, 1996. The air was electric that day, prompting Roger Peterson to say, "Man, I'm as nervous as when my kids were born." Bader replied, "Yeah, but when your kids were born, there wasn't the chance they'd blow up and kill you." From left to right are Mike Ball, Peterson, Matt Parks, Jere Peterson, Bader, and Craig Kenfield. *Victory*

The engine's mounting points (which triangulate the stress and load paths) were on the cylinder heads and at four points on the crankcase. It was also attached to the cradle at the base of the frame.

A British Flavor to Heads and Ports

Invaluable input on the port designs came from Mike Mills, an independent consultant from England whom Geoff Burgess had known for years and worked with previously. Mills had a wealth of experience as an engineer and designer, and his work on the Victory V-twin was significant because the port shapes and angles were among the most subjective aspects of the engine. It wasn't so much that there was a right or wrong way to design ports; rather, they're most aptly judged as being good, better, or best, and the Victory team deemed its port flow was among the best possible for that engine. Flow bench tests confirmed they had achieved highly effective flow through the heads.

"We decided Mike would do the initial [head] concept, especially for airflow," Burgess said. "Mike

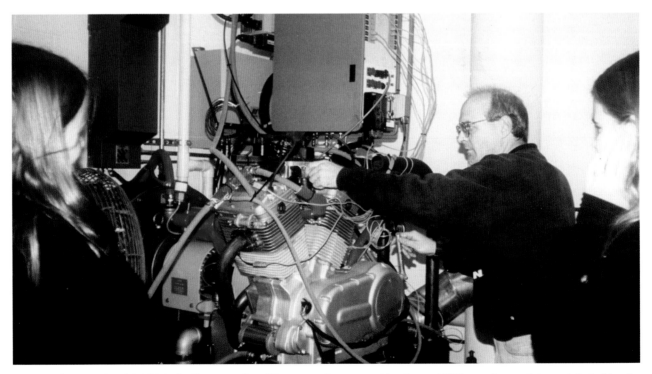

On Saturday, October 26, 1996, the first complete Victory engine ran on the dyno at 3:31 p.m. Once again, a string of long work days was required to get engine number C-1 up and firing. As Steve Weinzerl commented, "When you're building the first new American motorcycle to appear in 50 years, you put in a lot of 14-hour days." *Mark Bader*

The bizarre equipment mounted on this early production bike was used for sound testing. By heavily muffling the intake and exhaust noise, the potential for sound deadening could be determined. The odd canister mounted to the rear of the bike was hooked up to the exhaust pipe during testing. On the left side, a flexible aluminum tube runs from the intake to the front canister. *Victory*

would design where the valves went with the included angle, the size of the valves . . . and the port shapes to get the power that we needed."

Throughout the project, Mills presented his work in pencil drawings, not computer-aided design (CAD) illustrations. Burgess, for one, considered that to be a totally appropriate method of designing. Port design, according to Burgess, "is an interpretive, creative process . . . The [design station] only does what it's told. The individual has to come up with the better idea and from there it'll flow. And Mike said, 'This is the only way because I can rub it out and change it in two seconds,' and you can't do that with ProE [design software]."

(After work on the first engine, Mills grew familiar and comfortable with design software, which he used on future projects.)

Mills was more accustomed to working on ultra-high-performance engines, such as those for Kenny Roberts's racing team, than on street bikes. Yet, he found it easy to adapt his design approaches to the large-scale cruiser engine.

"Yes. What I know still applies here... All the knowledge you learn, it still applies, you're still seeking that efficiency of engine performance," he said. "But you Americans have a funny way of doing things. When you want to go faster, you make it bigger. There's too much mass with all these cruiser engines, but the layout is a marketing requirement. Without marketing input, my cruiser wouldn't look like this cruiser."

The patterns for the cylinder heads' castings (and the crankcases) were produced by Zeus Engineering, a British company whose clients include most Formula 1 race car teams. Among the key reasons Zeus was selected for the Victory project were its engineering know-how and rapid response time. The Victory team designed the heads, but got valuable feedback from

Parts for preproduction vehicles such as this old warhorse, PD-2, were made by creating a CAD drawing and sending it—along with a boatload of money—to a CNC house that turned the computer file into a finished part. Geoff Burgess shook his head and laughed while looking at PD-2, saying, "Can you believe it cost $250,000?" *Lee Klancher*

the Zeus staff, which helped to simplify the casting process. Bader spent several weeks in England with Mills in late 1996 as Zeus was creating the casting patterns. During this time, there was a free and productive exchange of ideas between vendor and Victory that hastened progress.

"There are places in the U.S. that could do the castings, but they would make exactly what we drew up, whereas Zeus would say 'we don't know if you want to do that,' so their expertise helped us," Bader said. "Plus, because they've got this racing background, they're very reactive and very quick on changes. They have to be. When a Formula 1 racing team comes in and says, 'We need these cylinder heads in three weeks,' it's not six months, it's three weeks."

EFI Survives Teething Problems

"EFI on four-strokes was totally new to Polaris," said Steve Weinzierl. Indeed, the company had previously used it only on snowmobiles, never even on ATVs,

The jumble of wires on the right was used to connect PD-2 to the sidecar rig for EFI testing. The gas tank was made of aluminum, and the engine side cover was an early unit quickly designed by Mark Bader and Matt Parks. The pop can was an economical preproduction breather catch tank. *Lee Klancher*

the division from which Weinzierl transferred to join the Victory team.

As Victory engineers and designers sorted out the V92C's EFI (electronic fuel injector), unfamiliarity with the new technology often made them long for good ol' carburetors, with jets and a mechanical makeup that they were oh-so-familiar with. Yet they forged on in the name of progress and developed—with help from a U.K. company called MBE, the electronic control unit (ECU) supplier—a highly effective fuel injection system.

The original EFI component supplier, whose ECU was used on the first concept bikes, withdrew suddenly in the midst of the project. The Victory team sought out alternate suppliers, though most were reluctant to sign on because of the incredibly short development schedule. But the MBE staff's background was in racing, where solutions are needed yesterday, and they welcomed the challenge.

"Jeff Moore of MBE was real helpful and I think it's been a perfect marriage between a vendor and Victory," Weinzierl said. Moore (the "M" of MBE) spent months with Victory team members in Wisconsin, Colorado (for high-altitude EFI calibration), and California, where he helped finalize calibrations before a preliminary emissions test.

The Victory team installed its first EFI setup on the "Hammer:" the raw, original Victory test engine (see sidebar). The engine got fuel, started, and ran, but in a sense, it was a case in which ignorance was bliss.

"Based on what we later learned about EFI, it's a miracle that engine ever started. It probably shouldn't have," Bader said.

In its production form, the Victory V92C EFI system fed the engine via 44mm throttle bores, one per intake port. Just how much fuel was supplied, and how fast, was controlled by the ECU (which is housed below the seat on the right side of the bike). The ECU wasn't a free-thinking brain, however; it was programmed with fuel maps that equipped it to respond instantly as conditions and fuel needs changed. Early fuel mapping was done with the V-twin on the engine dyno in Osceola. The second stage of mapping resulted from tests with the bike on a chassis dyno. (Both dynos were operated by Senior Development Technician Roger Peterson and Kevin

Hamann, who spent thousands of hours in the dyno room during V92C development.)

Final fuel map refinements were made on the road—literally. Here's a typical scenario of how the fuel calibrations were adjusted during field testing: With Weinzierl or Peterson riding the test bike, Moore—in a rough but functional Czechoslovakian sidecar—monitored fueling activity on a laptop computer. The laptop was wired to test equipment that included lambda sensors on both cylinders of the Victory engine. When a fuel supply inefficiency was detected, Moore altered the fuel mapping. Sometimes the adjustments were typed into the laptop on the fly, while other times—such as on rough or twisty roads—the driver pulled over so Moore could type

PD-2's dash was a jumble of parts-store gauges monitoring fuel and oil pressure, yellow temperature sensor leads, and CNC-manufactured perches and levers. Tuning notes were made on the strip of duct tape on the tank. The lead hanging from the right control was a throttle position sensor used for EFI testing. *Lee Klancher*

Once ready-state EFI tuning was finished on the dyno, this sidecar rig was used to tune the MBE fuel injection system in real-world conditions. Tuning an EFI system is no small task. Burgess estimated the team spent six months or more getting it right. *Lee Klancher*

with the bike parked. The test conditions were then duplicated to verify that the change was effective.

Among the many factors to which the ECU had to respond were altitude, driving styles (such as sudden or gradual changes in throttle position, both on and off the gas), and ambient operating temperatures. That's why extensive testing was done at high elevations and in desert heat.

The other element of the induction system, the Victory engine's air intake, was located above the engine, under the fuel tank. Thus, unlike most cruisers at the time, there was no side-mounted air cleaner. The intake's position was chosen for several reasons: to let the tank act as a shroud and slightly muffle intake noise, to provide the bike with clean styling and a unique look, and for performance.

"By not putting it on the side, we aren't copying anybody, and it seemed to be best for power because you have a down flow," Burgess said. "The intake

With Steve Weinzerl or Roger Peterson driving, Jeff Moore from MBE spent countless hours in this sidecar rig, using a laptop computer to adjust the ECU's fuel map. The fuel map is a set of programmed instructions that control how much fuel is supplied under varying conditions. The olive green lambda monitors display oxygen sensor readings. *Lee Klancher*

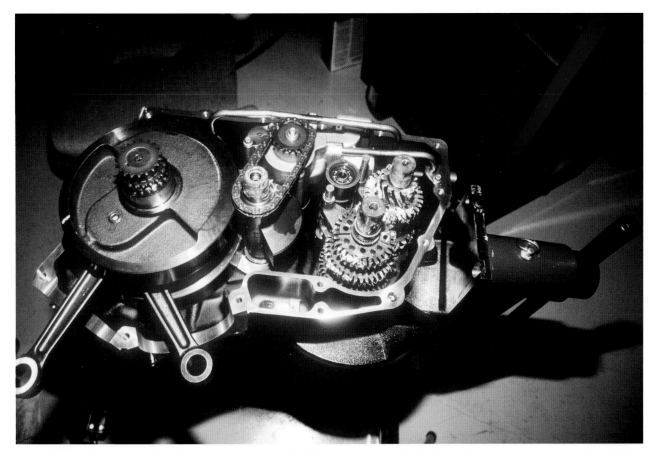

Mounted between the crankshaft and transmission, the Victory's balance shaft allowed the engine to vibrate just a bit, even though it could have been designed to eliminate nearly all vibration. Motorcycles need to have personality; a little rumble here and tingle there lets you know that the machine underneath you is alive and kicking. *Lee Klancher*

ports can be vertical like they should be, like on the Formula 1's, instead of coming from the side, where there's a ninety-degree bend into the port. But we had the typical design trade-off and conflict. We had to trade off the hole under the gas tank that eats up space for fuel, versus the minimum angle we needed to get air into the engine."

Cranking Out the Inertia

Two major considerations during crankshaft development were space constraints and the need to achieve a targeted level of inertia (an object's ability to maintain its motion). The team benchmarked crankshafts from numerous competitive motorcycles, measuring the inertia of each one and comparing that data to the particular bike's performance. The team then set inertia goals suitable for their engine's torque and horsepower goals.

"You can get inertia two ways, either by diameter or by width [of the crankshaft flywheels], so basically

when we dropped the crankshaft centerline down, that probably influenced the diameter we could get, so we added the width," said Burgess. "As you can see, the whole engine was evolving around these magic, key elements that, if you don't have them in the first place, you'll never get there."

Bader explained why a big flywheel was beneficial in a cruiser.

"In this cruiser market, a lot of times you have low-speed running, in-town running, and you want the engine to be easy to drive at low speeds. That big flywheel helps because it's less susceptible to stalling once you are going. You can basically sit there at no throttle and let it idle its way through traffic."

The size and shape of the crankshaft helped determine the crankcase size and, thus, overall engine size. The crankshaft connected directly to the balance shaft: an item that wasn't originally part of the plan, but which became vital.

The short piston used in conjunction with short rods to truncate the top end is visible in this cutaway engine displayed at dealer shows in the fall of 1997. The single overhead cam was selected to reduce the height of the engine. Dual overhead cams would have made the engine much higher. *Michael Dapper*

Striking a Balance and Changing Gears

When the Victory team decided to solid-mount the engine and make it a stressed member of the frame, they created more work for themselves.

They felt they *had* to solid-mount the engine because rubber-mounting would result in unacceptable frame and chassis flex. After all, one of their key goals had been a stiff, responsive-handling chassis; to permit the engine to shift about and flex the frame would have been self-defeating.

"If you draw a straight line from the steering head to the rear swingarm pivot, it goes right through the engine," said Matt Parks. "What's the strongest piece on the entire motorcycle? It's the engine, a big, huge hunk of aluminum. We said, 'Let's use this thing as a stressed member.'"

Solid-mounting the engine, however, meant the team had to account for the substantial vibration the engine would transmit throughout the bike. There *are* cruisers with solid-mounted engines and no apparatus to counter the vibrations, but benchmarking rides on such models had resulted in numb thighs and hands as shaky as an espresso addict's.

The Hammer

It was the summer of 1996, and the clock was ticking. The deadline for the Victory team to build and test its first engine was approaching. Parts were coming in from vendors, including the all-important cylinder heads, but the crankcases were running late and wouldn't arrive for another month. That was too long to wait, according to Mark Bader, who was then in charge of engine design.

"Instead of delaying the start-up of the engine, we came up with the idea of creating a simplified engine: no transmission, just the crankshaft, balance shaft, oil pump, and the output shaft. We quickly designed up a very simple crankcase and got a CNC [Computer Numerical Control] house to start hogging out big old chunks of aluminum."

What were those big old chunks of aluminum hogged out of? Out of an even bigger, enormous chunk of aluminum.

"The crankcase started out as a three-hundred-fifty-pound block of aluminum and it ended up weighing thirty pounds, so you figure out how many chips we ended up with," Bader said. "A lot of beer cans died for those cases."

Walls that would be 5mm thick on a production casting were as much as 20mm thick in the Hammer's cases. "You could light a bomb off inside of these things and not get hurt," Bader said.

The Victory staff worked long hours assembling the Hammer—as well as preparing the brand-new engine dyno. There were struggles with the engine, the dyno, and the mating of the two, prior to that highly anticipated first start-up.

Several 14-hour-plus days later, the crew finally believed the big day had arrived.

"I think we were zombies by that point," Bader said. "Mike Ball was turning the key and I was in the dyno cell; I think it was Roger (Peterson) and me standing in there. Roger turned to me and said, 'Man, I'm as nervous as when my kids were born.' And I said, 'Yeah, but when your kids were born, there wasn't the chance that they'd blow up and kill you.'"

The first time Ball tried starting the engine, it didn't fire. The team checked for spark and for fuel, and determined that the injection system had to be purged so the fuel would reach the injectors.

At 5:45 p.m. on Friday, September 6, 1996, Ball tried the starter again and the Hammer roared to life.

"It fired right up and I don't think there was a dry eye in the house," Bader said. "There were high fives and clapping and cheering. Probably what made it more emotional than it was, was that we were so doggone tired. It was an awesome feeling standing there. People were just dumbfounded."

The collective product of managers, engineers, and technicians—folks like Scott Walker, Danny Fredrickson, Kevin Hamann, Geoff Burgess, Matt Parks, Bader, Ball, and Peterson—had roared to life. It was a milestone, but one that came early on "The Road to Victory," as the team called it. The bike was far, far from finished, but what a thrilling step they had taken that fall Friday.

The answer was a balance shaft that would counter or neutralize the vibrations.

'Tuning' the Vibration

Believe it or not, some people like things that are imperfect, such as lumpy mashed potatoes, or, to be more germane, rumbling, vibrating motorcycles. Cruiser riders in particular don't want their bikes to be silent and vibration-free. There's some appeal (and an accompanying image) to a bike that literally makes the ground shake.

This desire for imperfection was an area where some Japanese cruisers failed: they were considered too technologically slick, too quiet or smooth-running, without soul, or even "like riding a Toyota Corolla" (which wasn't a compliment). The Victory team shared some of these views; some Japanese cruisers struck them as sterile and lacking in that desirable cruiser grittiness, while some Harley-Davidsons went too far the other direction.

That's why the team worked so hard on "tuning" the vibration *left in* the motorcycle. Mark Bader was familiar with balance shafts, which had been used on virtually every Kohler single, so he was comfortable designing one for Victory. But it worked too well,

The Victory team cast off the veil of secrecy surrounding its new machine on February 19, 1997, when a press release announced that Polaris would be entering the motorcycle market. Rumors had run rampant since the previous fall, but the press release was the first official acknowledgment of the bike's existence. *Lee Klancher*

in a sense, because it removed virtually *all* of the perceptible vibration.

In layman's terms, an engine produces countless vibrations of varying degrees, or frequencies. The only vibrations that merit attention are the first two levels, the primary (major) and secondary (minor) vibrations, because the others are practically negligible. Bader designed a balance shaft for the V92C that removed (or neutralized) virtually all of the primaries and some of the secondaries. The resulting ride of C-1, the team's first concept bike, was passionless; it had no soul.

To counteract this effect, Test Engineer Robin Tuluie did some theoretical analysis on Victory vibrations and the balance shaft. He produced data that showed the team needed to factor in chassis vibration and permit more primaries to surface.

"We had balanced it to what we thought would be perfect primary balance, so we had just our secondaries, and we really didn't like it," Bader said. "That's because the trick that the equations don't show is that the engine is solid-coupled to the chassis, and the chassis has its own natural frequency, or as a unit, [the bike] has a natural frequency. The primary balance that we were experiencing was exciting the natural frequency in the frame, and that made it feel worse than it was. So, by actually *im*balancing the engine more, or further from perfect, it felt better to the rider.

"The engine's producing more vibration but the rider doesn't feel more because the chassis isn't amplifying it."

The balance shaft proved versatile, as it drove the dual oil pumps and served as an intermediate shaft between the engine and the gearbox. "It's the basis of the gear reduction between the crankshaft and transmission," said Bader.

Originally, the transmission's primary drive was to be chain-driven, but the gear-drive setup was preferable because it proved more reliable over the life of the bike, and was considerably quieter than chain-drive.

On Any Sunday. . .

The introduction of Senior Project Engineer John Garms to the Victory project may be the best example of how tight the staffing and lead time were for this motorcycle. Garms arrived in Osceola on a Sunday—and started work that very day.

On June 26, 1997, the Victory was rolled out to the press at Planet Hollywood in the Mall of America in Bloomington, Minnesota. Flash bulbs popped, Al Unser Jr. rode a preproduction bike into the restaurant, and Victory team members fielded questions about the new bike. *Victory*

There was no "enjoy some cheese and a Packers game on TV and we'll see you Monday." No, it was more like: "This tranny needs work, can you come in today?"

Preliminary work on the V92C's five-speed gearbox had been done months earlier by non-Victory engineers in the Polaris Roseau facility. By the time Garms came on board in September 1996, the transmission was out of sync with the rest of the bike's development. Major reworking was required.

"We have changed everything except the number of teeth and the center-to-center distance," Garms said. "Everything else has changed, and there's in the neighborhood of one hundred thirty-five parts through the powertrain."

In the original design, durability of some drivetrain components was questionable, as was their ability to fit together. Garms was a good man to tackle the job, what with more than two decades of engine testing and development under his belt, including a stint at Harley-Davidson, where he was part of the team that developed the original Evolution engine. Before joining Victory, Garms worked for Cummins Diesel, where engines weren't measured in cc's but liters, as in the 45-liter V-12 he worked on before heading to Osceola.

The Victory powertrain consisted of: a gear-driven primary drive with a torque compensator; a large-diameter, multi-plate wet clutch; a five-speed gearbox

Led by Geoff Burgess (in light blue shirt, directly behind the bike), this group of people gave their all to the design and development of the V92C. At the time this photo was taken (January 25, 1998), the team focused on nailing down the final details before production started. *Lee Klancher*

with what could be considered oversized gears; and a belt-driven final drive.

The gears, clutch, and some other powertrain components were stout, probably beefier than necessary. That was for durability and reliability, but also because of the late restart on transmission development and the tight production schedule; with time, the team expected to make the powertrain lighter and more compact in future iterations. Garms estimated that some parts such as gears were 20 to 25 percent oversized, but he also noted that the team hadn't experienced a single gear train failure with the production-ready setup.

"Our gear train is even bigger than Harley-Davidson's, but we're going to be pulling twice the horsepower," Garms said. "At the horsepower level we're at, we have a robust design to handle the power. This is the flagship, the first vehicle, and it's felt that what we have today should handle all the horsepower requirements that are going to be asked of it. It fits the envelope, too—that 'shoe box' on the back of the engine."

The torque compensator smoothed out some of the engine's impulses that were transmitted back to the powertrain, and lessened gear train noise. In layman's terms, here's how the compensator operated: When the pistons went through their power strokes and the fuel/air mixtures were ignited, there were two firing impulses fairly close together. The torque compensator took the edge off those impulses, storing about 15 percent of each impulse in a spring-equipped mechanism, then returning the energy to the crankshaft as it rotated with the pistons' stroking.

"Our primary goals are to take this harshness off the gear train and lower the gear noise," Garms said.

A New Look at Braking

When developing an engine, dyno and road testing show whether you've achieved your goals. If you've got the horsepower and the true, usable power you sought, you're good to go.

But how do you measure or quantify something that's subjective, such as the way a bike's braking

This brochure featuring a very early CV bike was the first piece of promotional literature created for the bike. Note the tiny oil cooler and two bolts holding the fender to the rear subframe. The oil cooler would be enlarged significantly on production units, and the subframe would be lengthened, adding a third bolt to the rear fender. *Victory*

should feel? That was a challenge undertaken by Test Engineer Robin Tuluie. (*Dr.* Robin Tuluie, if you please; he received a doctorate in astrophysics.)

The Victory team had already subjectively evaluated competitors' brakes during benchmarking rides, so they knew which setups provided the feel and stopping power they desired. The challenge, though, was to determine whether they had achieved the desired performance in their own brake system.

Tuluie developed a way to apply instrumentation to a braking system so the team could quantify braking; they would apply numbers—figures that could be compared and analyzed—to measure braking feel and effectiveness.

"We liked using data acquisition because of riders' subjectivity," he said. "You design a [braking] system to fulfill the requirements, then test it again to see if it's really what you want."

After considering brake components from six suppliers, the Victory team tested systems from a couple companies and chose to use Brembo hardware. They assembled a brake system using a combination of

Brembo components that gave them the numbers—and feel—they wanted. Brembo technicians worked with the Victory team, and a Brembo test rider was particularly helpful in assisting the team's pursuit of the desired feel and responsiveness.

"We specified the system [to Brembo], and as much as possible, we tried to use off-the-shelf parts," Tuluie said. "Brembo doesn't make a master cylinder in the size we deemed best for the front brake, however, so we made up our own."

The braking feel the Victory team desired consisted of "linear" braking in front and digressive braking in the rear.

"For the front brake, we want it predictable, and if you pull it twice as hard, you want it to brake twice as hard," Tuluie said. "But you can lock up a rear brake, so you want to make a brake that stops the bike but doesn't lock up; as you push harder on it, you don't want it to decelerate quite as hard. For us, this was done by adjusting a certain lever geometry in the rear brake."

In the early stages of the Victory project, significant braking evaluation and testing was done on Francis

During the week of the press introduction at Planet Hollywood, select journalists were invited to visit the facility in Osceola, Wisconsin. A few were allowed to take the company's only prototype for test rides. Mark Tuttle Jr. of *Rider* magazine, shown riding the bike through the Osceola countryside, was told that if he dropped the bike, "You won't even hear the rifle shot." *Wayne Davis*

the Mule in Tennessee, using a test facility the team had in the Volunteer State. ("We eventually shut it down because people found out we were there," said Matt Parks. "At first it was great, it was a tiny town, but then people found out and we got to be big fish in a little pond. We'd come out and people would be waiting to see the bike.")

In production form, the front brakes consisted of a 300mm-diameter floating rotor with a four-

piston caliper. The rear brake had a 300mm-diameter floating rotor with a dual-piston caliper.

The V92C used 16-inch Dunlop tires mounted on 16-inch custom-made cast-aluminum wheels. The Victory script logo was cast into one of the five spokes of each wheel (on both sides of each wheel). The logo was positioned near the rim so it was visible just beyond the brake rotor on the front right and rear left sides of the bike.

Making Short Work of Long-Term Testing

Several test methods were used to evaluate the V92C's durability, including extended test rides between Osceola and the team's western test site. There were also engine durability tests consisting of 24-hour dyno tests at the Polaris facility in Roseau, and grueling sessions on special road-wear simulators.

Pre-production bikes underwent testing on simulators that recreated the rigors of road travel—in a hurry. Test Engineer Robin Tuluie said a Victory test bike mounted on the hydraulic ramps of an MTS Systems simulator endured the rigors of 30,000 miles of travel in just 10 days.

"The only thing that damages the chassis is a bump—a smooth road causes no damage—so the system cuts out all sections of smooth road [from its pre-recorded road input data]," Tuluie said. "You end up with an accelerated durability test that's approximately twenty times as short as it would take to perform this test on the road. The bike hits all the bumps of a two-hour ride in about ten minutes."

After a Victory test bike withstood 30,000 miles worth of abuse on the simulator, its failures were evaluated, yielding both good and bad news. While it was bad that they discovered *any* failures, the team found those problems to be the same as had been revealed from road testing, which gave them confidence in both test methods. Parts that failed were redesigned and the new parts were installed on a test bike that went through a test that simulated over 60,000 miles of bad roads.

"With the simulator, you find out everything from whether your mirrors are rattling to how good your seat is," said Matt Parks. "The only thing it doesn't have is engine vibration, and the thought is that if anything fails *without* engine vibration, it will certainly fail *with* engine vibration."

In another version of accelerated durability testing, bikes were driven on a proving ground test track that was so rough, one mile on the track was equivalent to five miles of road travel. The bikes were ridden hard on the track and they endured tremendous jarring, bumps, and vibrations.

A Well-Traveled Bike

The original Victory motorcycle project touched almost as many states as a vintage travel trailer. The go-ahead for the motorcycle project came from the Polaris corporate headquarters in Minneapolis, and initial engineering was done in Roseau before the Victory team moved to its engineering facility in Osceola, Wisconsin. (Engines were assembled at Osceola, and the complete motorcycle was assembled at the Polaris/Victory plant in Spirit Lake, Iowa.)

Developmental testing was done in several states, including Minnesota and Wisconsin, of course; Tennessee, where some early work was done, primarily with Francis the Mule; and Arizona, where the most significant benchmarking rides took place.

In Colorado, the electronic fuel injection (EFI) system was calibrated for various altitudes, and the team had a test facility in the south that was blessed by desert climate for year-round testing. It also gave them quick access to mountain elevations (on roads leading to the San Bernadino National Forest and Big Bear) and wide-open desert roads that provided, among other things, heat, fuel range, speed, and durability testing. Test bikes were also ridden, not trucked, between Wisconsin and California.

The original bike's components had varied origins as well. The forks were from Italian supplier Marzocchi; and from England came both the EFI's control unit from MBE and the cylinder heads and crankcases from Zeus Engineering.

Paint, Chrome, Logos and Leather

In final production form, the V92C looked remarkably clean, as if it were actually a prototype or show bike that didn't have all the necessary cables, hoses, and hardware of a real, running bike. There was little or no sign of the battery, cables, spark plug wires, air

The strip of duct tape on the tank is where Victory test riders recorded fuel usage, mileage, and any problems. Development technician Scott Dieltz records fuel consumption in a CV bike after a gas stop during testing on November 10, 1997. *Lee Klancher*

cleaner, or rear shock, yet everything was there, and the bike was not hiding all of these details under bodywork, *à la* a sport bike.

From the outset, the goal was to give the V92C a unique look, rather than make it a copycat of other cruisers on the road. To that end, Designer Dave Otto and G.M. Matt Parks put an emphasis on keeping the look clean rather than loading it up with covers, badges, and trim. The idea was to make the bike appealing and let its performance do the talking.

Testing in inclement weather was part of the process, although it was not always intentional. As his fellow test riders tried to figure out how to get off of the mountains before the rain turned to snow, Scott Dieltz looked in vain for a break in the sky. Things would get worse before they got better; heavy fog, steady rain, freezing temperatures, and rock slides would have the Victory test riders dodging boulders in near-zero visibility before the day was done.
Lee Klancher

Working from direction offered primarily by Parks, the Brooks Stevens design firm in Milwaukee produced the original concept drawings of the bike. The Victory team selected elements of those drawings that they liked, the concepts were refined, and the bike's look evolved. Throughout the project, Victory staffers offered input on assorted design and styling touches. Since virtually every member of the team was an avid and experienced motorcyclist, Parks took their input—likes, dislikes, and suggestions—to heart, and said "everybody in the group has their signature on that bike somewhere."

One Dave Otto touch: The headlight housing design was echoed in the design of the turn indicator housings, front and rear. Atop the headlight was the V92C's extensive instrumentation: a speedometer with a small tachometer at its base, and a small liquid-crystal display (LCD) panel that offered a collection of data (odometer, trip meter, clock, and fuel gauge). A rider could scroll through this data using a handlebar-mounted button, and could reset various functions using the button. The speedometer face also had several back-lit symbols (high-beam, turn-signal, low-oil, low-gas, and low-generator indicators).

The colors available for the first-year V92C paint were Antares Red and KYSO (Knock Your Socks Off) Blue. (Antares is an ancient, giant red star—the brightest in the constellation Scorpio.) The Victory script logo appeared in several places (wheel spokes, case covers, billet handlebar clamp), and the full-color Victory graphic appeared on the gas tank badge.

The Right Side of the Law

The Victory team received welcome cooperation when they were doing early development work in Roseau, Minnesota—the birthplace of parent company Polaris Industries—including some help from a local law enforcement officer.

This officer helped the team by monitoring via radio the location of a state highway patrol officer. This allowed test riders to do high-speed testing on a road near Roseau.

Who needs a radar detector when there's a local officer on hand to monitor the smokey's location by radio?

Making First Impressions

[Editor's Note: This sidebar appears as it originally did in The Victory Motorcycle, *published in 1998.]*

No matter how good a motorcycle the Victory team developed, the bike would go nowhere without an effective promotional effort. Judging by preproduction interest in the bike as this book went to press, the effort has been a success, and demand for Victory motorcycles will likely outstrip supply for a couple models' years— at least.

The first official word of the Victory project came when Polaris announced on February 19, 1997, that it was entering the motorcycle market. The announcement came in a press release distributed by the company's public relations agency, Shandwick USA. The release was accompanied by a color photo of the Victory logo, but not the motorcycle.

The First Ride

The Osceola, Wisconsin, municipal airport isn't known for its aviation firsts. But it *was* home to history of another sort—the motorcycling kind—on November 7, 1996, when the first Victory concept bike was ridden on its runway.

A group of 18 people, including Victory team members, Polaris corporate executives, and a couple selected friends of executives, gathered on the rural runway to see, hear, and feel the company's new baby. Everything went fine, and although there wasn't much of an opportunity to experience the bike's responsive handling, some riders did push the bike to triple digits by the end of the airstrip.

Despite the small crowd and remote location, spy photos were taken.

"Some guy who had landed his plane at the airport saw this unique bike that was running up and down the runway at one hundred miles an hour," said Matt Parks. "He's thinking, 'What's up with that?' Next thing you know, he's out there with this gigantic long lens, snapping spy pics. They never made it to magazines, fortunately. But they made it to some dealers."

The bike made its public debut at the Planet Hollywood restaurant at the Mall of America in Bloomington, Minnesota, on June 26, 1997. Indy car racer Al Unser, Jr., rode the bike into the packed restaurant to give the gathered media, Polaris staffers, and invited guests their first look—and listen.

The following day, editors from several motorcycle magazines met the Victory staff in Osceola, Wisconsin, to learn more about the bike and, for a select few, take it for a first-impression ride. The result was universally positive reviews from the motorcycle press. It also received coverage in newspapers such as the *Wall Street Journal*, *New York Times*, and *USA TODAY*, and General Manager Matt Parks appeared on television on CNN and CNBC.

A couple of V92Cs were on display at the annual Sturgis rally in August 1997, and they were running models of near-production quality, not just show bikes. They laid down some rubber on the Main Street of Sturgis during the rally week.

A Victory website was launched in the summer of '97, and the first group of U.S. Victory dealers was announced in mid-November of that year. Show bikes drew crowds at motorcycle shows throughout the fall and winter, and the first Victory dealer convention was held in January 1998 in Palm Springs, California.

The public got its first chance to ride the new motorcycle on demo rides at Daytona Bike Week in March 1998, and production models were scheduled to roll out of the Spirit Lake production plant in the spring of 1998.

This side view of an early Victory production bike was taken in the summer of 1997. Although this bike is quite complete, the Victory received a host of subtle but significant changes before being released to the public. *Wayne Davis*

CHAPTER 2

A Victory Historical Overview

The early days of Victory Motorcycles are covered in chapter 1. The focus in this chapter is to trace the brand's history from mid-1998 to Victory's final year in business.

The introduction of the V92C generated tremendous excitement. The motorcycle world was thrilled to have a new manufacturer enter the business, especially one with the manufacturing acumen and fiscal stability of Polaris.

In the days after the June 26, 1997, V92C introduction at the Mall of America in suburban Minneapolis, several motorcycle journalists got to test ride the V92C prototype. It received mostly positive reviews, but the editors of *Cycle World* offered critical notes about a handful of design or performance issues. The Victory product development team assured the *Cycle World* reps those issues would be addressed before the bike went into production. Later that year, *Cycle World* named the V92C "Best Cruiser" for 1998. But years later, one editor noted that Victory did *not* make those changes, upsetting some *Cycle World* staff members.

A Victory dealer network was quickly established. Many of the northern dealers were Polaris snowmobile or ATV dealers, and only some of them sold motorcycles. But considering Harley-Davidson's sales success at the time and the overall demand for American heavyweight motorcycles, many Victory dealers thought the new bikes would practically sell themselves and generate easy, impressive profits.

Consumers placed deposits on V92Cs and the first 1,500 units would be "numbered bikes" (minus bikes No. 2–14, which were given to company directors and management), with the final four numbers of the VIN etched on an oval plate placed atop the handlebar bracket.

Eager consumers placed those deposits and then they, and their Victory dealers, waited. Unfortunately, there were delays in the delivery of components, and no bikes had been produced by early summer 1998. But the Spirit Lake, Iowa, final assembly facility was ready to roll, so a team of about a dozen employees went into the plant on the Fourth of July and built the first V92C production unit. By building that Antares Red and Black V92C, they gave Victory an historic and memorable birthday. The group built one bike, then shut down the line, relocked the building, and went off to their respective holiday celebrations.

Bike No. 1

That first bike had a brief but eventful road history. About 10 days after it was built, the bike was ridden by a relay team of riders to each of the Polaris

Early Victory prototypes were tested all over the United States. Winter testing was conducted at a rented garage near Palm Springs, California. These late prototypes were being tested in the Palm Springs area in November 1997.
Lee Klancher

facilities in Iowa, South Dakota, Minnesota, and Wisconsin. A plant manager at each site signed a document commemorating the ride. The first leg of the relay ride ran from Spirit Lake to Polaris corporate headquarters in Medina, Minnesota. That sent the bike (ridden by then-project engineer Mario Negri) up Minnesota Hwy. 169—and right past the Excelsior-Henderson (EH) offices and factory in Belle Plaine, Minnesota.

The long-cherished version of the story is that Negri laid down an impressive burnout in the EH parking lot before continuing north. Ten years after the ride, Negri denied it, saying with a laugh: "I think we just did a fly-by, but if it makes the story more interesting, go ahead and say we did some burn-outs."

But, to the delight of Victory riders, there is confirmation of the burnout. James Holroyd, long an invaluable member of the Victory engineering team during the brand's history, was a design engineer for EH in 1998. He confirms that Victory rubber was laid down in Belle Plaine.

"Yep, it was done," Holroyd said. "The bike was ridden through the Excelsior-Henderson parking lot, a burnout was done, and much smack was talked inside the building."

Following the relay tour to Polaris sites, V92C No. 1 was put on display in the Victory Grille, the employee restaurant inside Polaris corporate headquarters. The relay was probably the bike's last run. It was wheeled outside the building for a 2004 photo shoot conducted by this book's author, but it was not available as desired for the model year 2009 dealer meeting held in Las Vegas in late July 2008. The plan was to have No. 1 ridden on stage along with a 10th Anniversary Victory Vision. But company officials ordered the technical services team not to revive the long-dormant first bike. Instead, V92C No. 5, owned by then-Polaris CEO Tom Tiller, was ridden onstage in Vegas.

The First 1,500

Of the first 1,500 V92C units produced—the "numbered bikes"—the lowest numbered were given to company directors and upper management. The consumers who filled out the remainder of the count to 1,500 didn't immediately take delivery of bikes in 1998, but they did

Here is the commemorative number plate atop the handlebar clamp on V92C No. 1. Each of the first 1,500 Victory motorcycles built had similarly numbered plates. *Author*

Photographed in the Spirit Lake plant with the first production unit were Polaris executives (l-r with their 1998 titles): CEO W. Hall Wendel, Jr., incoming President Tom Tiller, Victory General Manager Matt Parks, and outgoing President Ken Larson. *Victory*

receive a copy of the book, *The Victory Motorcycle*. Due to production delays—only 1,155 units were built in the 1998 calendar year—buyers received their books long before they got their bikes.

A factory employee at the time noted that along with component delays, the early stages of production progressed slowly because the entire team was so committed to producing a top-quality product. "We were trying to make sure these were going to be good units," the employee said.

Most of the numbered bikes were shipped in 1999. The first 1,500 were a mix of Antares Red and Black with gold pinstripes, and KYSO—Knock Your Socks Off—Blue and Black with gold pinstripes. Many numbered bikes still exist. With the Victory division's

shutdown, bike No. 1 was expected to be moved from Medina to the visitors' center (completed in August 2017) at the Spirit Lake facility. CJ Stephens, neither a Polaris dealer nor an executive, owns and rides No. 14. He also owns bike No. 16, which has long been displayed at Gregory Polaris, an outstanding dealership in Jacksonville, Arkansas. Dean Cross, who previously owned a Minnesota dealership called Warner Outdoor, owns and still rides No. 22.

In late 1998, Frank Marvin, then-vice chairman of Marvin Windows in Warroad, Minnesota, purchased V92C No. 13 as a sign of support for Polaris, which was founded (and still thrives to this day) in Roseau, 22 miles from the window factory. For years, he displayed the bike in the living room at his home, causing his wife Margaret "mild shock," he joked, at the time he bought the bike. The bike is now in the collection at The Shed, a Warroad car museum.

In 1998, Mark Klein owned a Ducati and Victory motorcycle dealership in Manhattan. His father Joe, a former sprint car racer who was always up for a challenge, wanted to help promote Mark's store, so in October 1998, he made the "Rock to Rock" ride across the United States on KYSO Blue V92C No. 39. Joe had a support driver with him, so it wasn't a grueling race across the country, but he was the first to ride from Manhattan to the San Francisco piers facing The Rock, Alcatraz. (In 2000, Joe was the first to post a speed run time on the Bonneville Salt Flats on a V92SC. He hoped to also run his No. 39 on the salt, but its tires weren't rated for competition, and it didn't pass tech inspection.)

Seeking Momentum

The combination of production delays, the newness of some dealerships to the motorcycle business, and the public's underwhelmed impression of the product kept the Victory fuse unlit in the brand's first few years in business. If bikes had been in dealerships earlier in 1998 to capitalize on the tremendous buzz and interest generated throughout the second half of 1997, things might have been different.

But instead, the V92C rolled into dealerships in late 1998 and early 1999, and dealers quickly learned they truly had to *sell* the bikes; they weren't being snatched up at above-MSRP premium prices as envisioned. The dealers who achieved success were primarily those who knew the motorcycle business and were truly engaged—they rode, talked, loved, and lived motorcycles. Dealers who were focused on snowmobiles and ATVs—or lawn and garden equipment or hardware—likely dusted the V92Cs in their showrooms countless times.

Early adopters, the riders who eagerly bought the newest brand on the road, were often seeking brand association that projected the image of "different" and "unique" instead of the "me too" of riding a Harley. Many riders sought out Victory dealerships after being insulted or ignored in Harley dealerships. These riders told of telling a Harley salesman "I'm just looking," and being told to "come back when

Victory knew the best way to sell bikes was to get people on them through demo rides. The brand spent millions of dollars on its demo ride program over the years, and had as many as five trucks such as this on the road to provide free rides. *Author*

you're ready to buy"—or worse—and then abandoned by the salesman.

Early Victory sales were strongest in the Upper Midwest and the Northeast, regions where Polaris was familiar to powersports enthusiasts. Sales were also "good, not great" in Florida and parts of Texas. Unfortunately, the brand never gained great traction in Southern California, nor in Chicago. Strong dealers such as Arlen Ness produced decent sales numbers in Northern California, but these assessments are extremely relative: there were single, high-profile Harley-Davidson dealers who sold more bikes in a year than an entire region of Victory dealers.

In an attempt to make news and spark sales, Victory in late 1999 introduced the V92C SE, a limited edition (only 400 were to be built) with laced wheels, a small "Superfly" windshield, and pulled-back handlebars. The brand also introduced the 2000 V92SC, the SportCruiser (covered in chapter 3), that same year. This big-forked model didn't rekindle the brand's momentum, so in mid-2000, Victory introduced the V92C Deluxe. The Deluxe was accessorized to become a bagger (leather saddlebags, windshield, studded driver seat, passenger backrest). It still wasn't a game-changer, and Victory idled along, with strong dealers selling bikes, and casual dealers selling one, two, maybe three units in a year and wondering why things weren't going better.

Victory reworked and restyled its engine, tweaked the transmission, and for model year 2002 introduced its new Freedom engine, which powered every 2002 model. The lineup that year included two new models, the V92TC—the Touring Cruiser—and a TC Deluxe. The TC featured the second Victory project work by then-industrial designer Mike Song: the stylish hard saddlebags. The new engine earned good reviews from the motorcycle press, while at the same time, some early Victory owners with pre-Freedom drivetrains were experiencing transmission issues.

A True Game-Changer

For the 2003 model, Victory introduced a *true* game-changer, the Victory Vegas. The bike reflected the willingness and desire of the second-generation Victory leadership team—GM Mark Blackwell, Product Manager Gary Laskin, Song, and a revamped engineering team—to step far outside the retro cruiser box with an all-new model featuring modern and progressive design. It also reflected the team's ability to produce outstanding motorcycles.

The motorcycle world didn't abandon Harley-Davidson for the smooth and sleek Vegas, but the bike sold well and gave Victory an incredibly versatile platform. Blackwell pledged that the brand would introduce at least one new model every year, and the run had begun. In consecutive model years, Victory introduced the TC, Vegas, Kingpin, Hammer, Jackpot, Kingpin Tour (okay, add an asterisk to this "new" model), and then the Victory Vision.

Then-Industrial Designer Mike Song, photographed in his office in 2004 with the first Victory Vegas fuel tank, designed the award-winning bike. Its unique tank had a raised spine and split tail integrated with the front of the driver seat. *Author*

In the midst of this run, in the fourth quarter of the 2005 fiscal year, Victory showed a profit for the first time. There was light at the end of the tunnel, but to stick with that metaphor, the tunnel was long, and it ran uphill. Victory was producing tremendous motorcycles through the first decade of the new century, but the brand was chasing a cultural phenomenon, Harley-Davidson.

Still, riders who bought Victory motorcycles loved them. In December 2006, J.D. Power and Associates announced that Victory had earned the highest ratings in three of five categories in its new motorcycle buyers' satisfaction survey. Victory received the highest-possible five "Power Circles" (i.e., stars) in product performance, service experience, and cost of ownership. The brand earned four of five circles in quality and sales experience.

But it would require more of Victory than excellent motorcycles to gain meaningful market share.

What Went Right

Polaris wasn't in the charity business. It operated the Victory division for roughly 20 years because of the brand's potential, products, and revenue. Eventually, the revenue and motorcycle market share didn't make fiscal sense to company leadership, and the brand's wind down was announced in early 2017.

Yes, Victory struggled to produce the numbers needed to sustain a business, but Victory also did a lot of things right. It has already been made clear—and is only reinforced throughout the following individual model coverage—that your author holds these bikes in the highest regard. Victory produced outstanding motorcycles. Period. Plus, the division always had outstanding leadership and the brand made valiant efforts at marketing—both of which, are reviewed in this chapter.

Everything learned and produced in Victory's history has set Polaris up for tremendous success with Indian Motorcycle. While Indian technology is intentionally different from that of Victory (for the purpose of making each brand distinct), Victory DNA is present throughout the Indian lineup as of model year 2017. Victory owners will surely scrutinize forthcoming Indian models to judge whether those bikes were originally developed for Victory and then rebranded for Indian post-January 9, 2017. If Indian introduces a touring bike with a high-performance liquid-cooled engine in the near future, Victory social media sites will explode anew. *That* was the bike Victory riders were eagerly awaiting.

Leadership

Victory did not lack for skilled, experienced leadership. Matt Parks was the brand's first general manager (GM) and he, along with original chief engineer Geoff Burgess, largely directed the makeup of the V92C and V92SC. Parks assumed leadership of Victory after having been the Polaris ATV product manager. He was an avid motorcyclist, and the SportCruiser in particular was a product of his vision for a high-performance cruiser. He went on to become a Polaris *RZR* off-road racing champion.

After Parks left Polaris, then-president of Polaris (and later CEO) Tom Tiller filled in as Victory's GM. Tiller was a long-time powersports enthusiast, and his pre-Polaris resume included serving as a division chief at General Electric under an American business icon of the time, CEO Jack Welch. After leaving Polaris, he was a top executive for companies in the solar energy and home décor industries.

In September 2000, Mark Blackwell became Victory's GM. Blackwell had been a motocross racing champion, then led business divisions at American Suzuki Motor Corp. before becoming vice president, sales and marketing, at the Polaris rival, Arctic Cat. Blackwell was inducted into the AMA Motorcycle Hall of Fame in 2000, and in 2013, was honored as an AMA Motorcycle Hall of Fame Legend. He oversaw the Victory division as it rolled out a steady succession of new models, and near the end of his 13-plus years with Polaris, Blackwell was vice president of international business and special projects.

In May 2009, Steve Menneto took the helm at Victory. The powersports business was his life. His family ran a Polaris dealership in upstate New York, and he and his brother Mike grew up helping their dad at the store. Mike succeeded his father as head of the dealership while Steve shifted to the corporate side in 1997, when he became a Polaris district sales manager. He rose steadily through the ranks, becoming director, North American sales, before assuming

Victory demo trucks provided free demo rides at rallies, such as Americade 2012 shown here, and at Victory dealerships. *Author*

the lead role in the motorcycle division. As this book goes to press, Menneto is Polaris president, motor-cycles, overseeing Indian Motorcycle, Slingshot, and Victory.

Menneto recognized the power of a legendary brand, and he and Polaris CEO Scott Wine were the primary proponents of the company acquiring the assets of Indian Motorcycle. Polaris announced the acquisition in 2011, and introduced the highly successful new generation of Indian bikes at the Sturgis rally in August 2013.

Marketing

It can be debated at length whether Victory marketing and advertising were effective, but there's no denying the brand's tremendous marketing efforts and investment over the years. While its revenue didn't compare to that of larger international competitors (H-D, Honda, Yamaha, etc.), Victory invested in high-profile exhibits and displayed at motorcycle shows all across North America and in Europe.

Victory also advertised extensively in motorcycle media and ran commercials on motorsports broadcasts such as stock car racing. The brand financed the building of custom bikes for display at shows and rallies, and to reinforce Victory's high-performance image, Victory invested in race bikes and teams that competed at Pikes Peak, the Isle of Man, and in NHRA. The high-performance message was also promoted through the brand-financed Victory Stunt Team, which performed at the Sturgis and Daytona rallies and select other events.

Darcy Betlach was the brand's second marketing manager and an innovative, creative force. Her family was immersed in motorcycling and the motorcycle business, so she grew up with legends such as Arlen Ness and Donnie Smith as family friends. With Victory in 2000, she connected the brand with the extremely popular (regionally) Minnesota Vikings. Victory became the official motorcycle of the Vikings, and Mascot Ragnar rode a custom-painted V92C onto the field before home games. Polaris hosted a "Vikings Day" at its corporate HQ in the fall of 2000, and Ragnar rode the bike through the halls of the office building.

Betlach also got Victory connected with Richard and Kyle Petty of NASCAR, and Victory became the official motorcycle and a participating sponsor in the Kyle Petty Charity Ride for several years. Betlach understood loyalty marketing: she started distribution of a Victory magazine for owners and launched the Victory Riders Association (VRA), an owner loyalty group. Victory annually hosted Victory bike owner parties at rallies in Daytona and Sturgis, and gave owners custom lapel pins or other branded swag at each of these events. Victory also provided modest support to the independent Victory Motorcycle Club (VMC) for activities such as the V2V Relay and its National Meet.

Victory marketing managers always understood that the bikes had to do the talking—and selling—so Victory operated an aggressive demo ride program

for most of its history. Initially, the brand's single demo truck offered rides at motorcycle rallies across the country. As time passed, more trucks were added, and in the brand's final 10 years there were multiple trucks—five at the program's peak—staging demo days at rallies and at Victory dealerships across North America. (Indian Motorcycle operates a similar demo ride program at rallies and dealerships.)

Victory's connections to celebrities were modest, at best. Comedian Tom Arnold made a few appearances at bike shows and rode a Victory on *The Best Damn Sports Show* on the Fox Sports Network, but it was comedic and not a purely positive promotion.

But Victory marketing hit the bull's-eye around 2012 when it hired actor R. Lee Ermey, "The Gunny," to represent the brand, especially in its military outreach efforts. Gunny, a Marine Corps veteran whose greatest fame came from his performance in the 1987 film, *Full Metal Jacket*, was a tremendous hit at public appearances and on video for Victory.

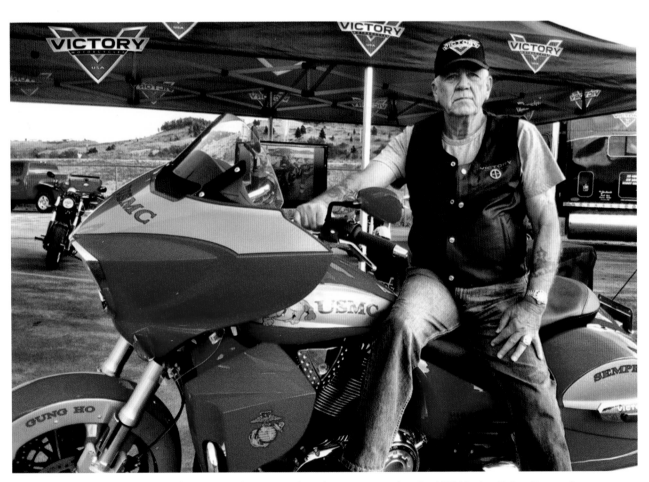

The most effective celebrity spokesperson Victory employed was actor and retired US Marine R. Lee Ermey, known as "The Gunny" for his iconic role in the film *Full Metal Jacket*. *Victory*

Your author worked with him at rallies, bike shows, and events such as Rolling Thunder in Washington, D.C. Ermey's enduring appeal was undeniable. He really rode Victory motorcycles and he passionately promoted the bikes and the brand.

For its lack of profitability, Victory was a generous supporter of worthy causes. Victory donated to Victory Junction, the outstanding camp Kyle Petty founded for children with illnesses and challenges, and supported military personnel organizations such as Operation Gratitude, Wounded Warriors, and Iraq and Afghanistan Veterans of America (IAVA).

One, oh, let's say *curious* promotional effort was when Victory teamed with Playboy for the model year 2013 brochure. The new-bike photo shoot was conducted at the Playboy Mansion in Los Angeles, with three playmates posing in Victory apparel with the bikes. Why? To support Operation Gratitude, according to a message in the brochure: "Joining forces with another iconic American brand, we teamed up with Playboy to support the military men and women who serve our nation around the world." But at the 2012 Sturgis rally, the three playmates conducted an autograph session at the Victory display in downtown Sturgis. Unfortunately for them, Gunny was signing autographs there at the same time; while he attracted the usual long line of fans, the Playmates drew only a few curious bystanders.

What Went Wrong

For Victory riders, Victory dealers, and Polaris employees, 8:15 on the morning of January 9, 2017, was a "Where were you?" moment. That was when Polaris publically issued a statement—and informed employees gathered in its facilities—announcing it was "winding down its Victory Motorcycles brand and related operations." The company pledged to help dealers sell their motorcycle inventory, and said it would make parts available for 10 years. The company statement included a quote from Chairman and CEO Scott Wine:

"This was an incredibly difficult decision for me, my team and the Polaris Board of Directors. Over the past eighteen years, we have invested not only resources, but our hearts and souls, into forging the Victory Motorcycles brand, and we are exceptionally proud of what our team has accomplished. Since inception, our teams have designed and produced nearly sixty Victory models that have been honored with twenty-five of the industry's top awards. The experience, knowledge, infrastructure and capability we've built in those eighteen years gave us the confidence to acquire and develop the Indian Motorcycle brand, so I would like to express my gratitude to everyone associated with Victory Motorcycles and celebrate your many contributions."

Dealers were stunned, most employees were shocked (only a few had advance notice of the move), and Victory riders were stunned, shocked, *and* livid. They lit up social media, especially in the Victory Motorcycle Owners group on Facebook. Riders couldn't understand how, or why, but several factors were nails in Victory's coffin, including these:

Engines: The Freedom engine was aging and would need updating to comply with upcoming stricter European standards. A liquid-cooled V-twin was reportedly under development, but it was a big engine that wouldn't suit every model. (Considering its development costs and progress, it's expected that this engine will be reworked for use in Indian models.)

Sales: Research shows Victory manufactured about 135,000 bikes in its 18-plus years of production. About 1,155 bikes were built in the first partial year of production (1998), and as of May 1, 2005, 18,240 bikes had been built, an average of 2,280 per year. For model year 2006, the build was 7,930 units, and production peaked in 2012, when about 14,000 units were built—led by the strong-selling Cross bikes (primarily the Cross Country and Cross Country Tour).

Those numbers don't offer much hope of profitability and didn't earn Victory much market share. It's not a fair comparison, but consider the elephant Victory was chasing: in 2016 alone, Harley-Davidson reported selling 161,658 motorcycles in the United States, and a total of 260,289 worldwide—versus 135,000 for Victory's entire history.

In Victory's final years, global and U.S. heavyweight cruiser markets were shrinking, yet Polaris had two brands, Victory and Indian, competing for market share. The Polaris directors concluded they would shutter Victory and compete full throttle with Indian, whose sales were growing steadily.

Profitability: Victory did not show a profit until the fourth quarter of 2005. That's about nine years in business, all in the red. Without the fiscal strength of Polaris, Victory would have been shuttered years earlier. (See: Excelsior-Henderson of the 1990s and early 2000s.) The Victory team celebrated in 2005, and numerous employees received plaques commemorating the profitable quarter. But it didn't last; as Vision development costs mounted, profitability became a more daunting challenge. Developing the Vision cost in the neighborhood of $22–24 million, and with those costs amortized over a five-year period, that extra $5 million annual nut for a single touring model was likely enough to make profitability unfeasible at that time.

With the enhanced wisdom of hindsight, rhetorical questions can be posed: What if the versatile, more traditional-looking Cross bikes had been introduced before the Vision? Would it have positioned Victory better to succeed?

And in its final years, Victory was essentially underwriting new-bike sales. Sales team members said of those years, "Every time we sold a new bike, it cost us fifteen hundred dollars" because rebates, discounts, or other costly promotions were always being offered.

The Power of the Brand

Here's a simple way to measure brand appeal: Would you buy a T-shirt with a company's logo if you didn't ride that brand of motorcycle? For Triumph, Indian Motorcycle, and Harley-Davidson, the answer is yes; people who will never throw a leg over a motorcycle seat buy and wear these brands' apparel because it conveys the message, "Cool." They want to be identified with these brands.

The Victory brand never achieved that cachet, understandably. Comparatively, Victory was a young brand. It hadn't sent bikes to war, and hadn't raced on board tracks, flat tracks, and road courses. It hadn't

been featured in movies like *Easy Rider*, hadn't been ridden by countless celebrities, and hadn't been the bike of choice for the early Hells Angels. (However, legendary Angels leader Sonny Barger rides a Victory, as do his wife and an impressive number of West Coast Angels.)

Victory made outstanding motorcycles and invested heavily in marketing and promotion, but you can't manufacture brand power. You cannot force appeal. It must be earned over time and by accomplishment. Or, it must be powered by the public embracing the brand and wanting to identify with it.

Remember the words of former Polaris executive Bob Nygaard, whose research helped the company decide to enter the motorcycle business: "Let me sell against price, let me sell against features and benefits, let me sell against more advertising, and I can find ways to do that," he said as Victory was launched. "[But h]elp me to sell against the lifestyle, with loyalty that is as passionate as I've ever seen on any product, i.e., Harley-Davidson. To sell against an image is very, very difficult, and that was my biggest concern."

Countless riders who owned other brands of bikes took Victory demo rides and were mightily impressed. The Victory demo bike was faster, handled better, and was more comfortable than their Harley or VTX. But that enthusiasm for the bike didn't often enough carry over to the dealership. Not enough riders could make the leap to a brand that wasn't Harley, which their family and friends had ridden for years. These hesitant riders chose to stick with— and be identified with— the brand they knew to be resilient and powerful. They rejected the better bike, the Victory, because the brand wouldn't give them the powerful, popular identity they sought.

And that proved fatal to Victory.

The End

Around Thanksgiving 2016, Victory assembly line workers in the Spirit Lake facility shut down the line and headed home for an extended break. They knew production would be suspended until early January for scheduled work on the plant's paint system, and that improvements would be made to the Victory assembly line.

The ignoble end for Victory at the Sturgis rally came with this modest 2017 display. A far cry from the lively Victory displays of earlier years, a single bike parked under an unmanned 10×10 pop-up tent represented the brand. *Author*

Five partially assembled bikes were left on the Victory line during the break. They would be completed in early January 2017, after employees returned to the plant and heard the shocking news that Victory had 18 months to live. A red Vegas was the last bike ever to come off the Victory line at 9:36 a.m. on Jan. 10, 2017.

At International Motorcycle Shows (IMS) in early 2017, Polaris shrank the Victory display and staffed it with an employee or two who would offer: (1) gratitude to loyal Victory owners, and (2) the company's official statement on the brand's wind down. At the first post-announcement IMS, in Dallas, a security plan was in place to safely evacuate the Victory employee(s) if consumers posed a physical threat. *That's* how upset Victory owners were with the Polaris decision. (No violence materialized at the Dallas show, nor at subsequent events.)

A collection of about a dozen Victory models were on display (and some of them were sold on-site) at Daytona Bike Week in March 2017. By then, Victory loyalists had calmed considerably, and discussions with the Victory staffers at the rally were civil.

The 2017 Sturgis rally included what might have been Victory corporate's final public presence. Parked almost unnoticed under a 10×10-foot pop-up tent was a lone Victory. It was originally a white Magnum X-1, but observers opined that it was better looking than the Indian models nearby, so it was replaced by a black High-Ball.

On nearby Lazelle Street and Junction Avenue, Victory owners from across the country experienced the rally and toured the Black Hills. They knew how long they would ride their favorite bikes: 'til the wheels fall off.

CHAPTER 3

Early Models: V92C Variants

Victory made outstanding cruisers. Each one had impressive power and delivered a great ride with smooth, intuitive handling. That sounds like advertising copy, but it's true. They were absolutely a blast to ride.

Victory cruisers might not be everyone's top picks, but virtually every rider would have to admire their ride quality. The solid-mounted engine helped create a rigid, no-flex platform that tracked on a true, consistently predictable line through corners.

Along with industrial designers like Mike Song, credit Victory engineers for creating these outstanding bikes. You could climb on any one of them and immediately ride hard with confidence. A Victory product manager could ask for anything—a wide rear tire, a wide rear tire and a tall front wheel, a bike with ape hangers, a sporty cruiser—and the engineering team delivered.

Victory models produced before the Vegas was introduced are covered in this chapter.

V92C

The development of the original Victory model, the V92C, is covered in chapters 1 and 2. Here we'll look at how the bike performed and what it was like to ride.

Compared to Victory cruisers that followed, starting with the Vegas, the V92C had a traditional upright riding position. Its seat height was 28 inches and you sat *on* the bike, not *in* it as you did on bikes like the Vegas and Kingpin. The V92C was a solid bike, with a rigid-mounted engine that strengthened the frame, stout forks, and Brembo brakes you could count on. The engine provided good power and was reliable with its electronic fuel injection, counter balancer, and oil circulation to assist in the cooling.

The original transmission, however, was an issue. It shifted loudly (which led to a raft of complaints) and it had performance issues. For 2001, the transmission was improved, but on many bikes, third gear was too hard and it could shatter. In 2006, Polaris issued a safety recall that addressed the too-hard third gear of the second-generation transmissions with a "cush drive" kit. The company supplied them to bike owners long, long after their bikes were out of warranty—even 10 years after riders bought their bikes. In part, the recall notice said:

This studio shot from the 2000 Victory brochure shows a bike with a tall (for Victory) seat height of 28 inches, and controls positioned to create a traditional riding position. Going forward, Victory continued to route both exhaust pipes on the right sides of most early models, but the driver seat height was lowered significantly. *Victory*

For the 2001 brochure photo shoot, this V92C was actually attached to a truck via a stout, side-mounted tow bar; the bar was Photoshopped out of the final image. However, the riding model turned the bars *into* the turn instead of countersteering. *Cycle World* called Victory out on this inaccurate portrayal of how to control a bike. *Victory*

"The Victory Motorcycle Division of Polaris Industries Inc. has decided that a defect which relates to motor vehicle safety exists in some model year 2001 and in some 1999–2000 motorcycles that received transmission replacement kits built in 2001... Some model year 2001 Victory V92 motorcycles, and some 1999–2000 V92 motorcycles if they received a transmission replacement kit built in 2001, can experience a third gear failure if an abnormal overload condition occurs such as when shifting at high RPM. If third gear fails, pieces of the gear could become lodged in the transmission; the transmission could lock up, possibly resulting in loss of control and a vehicle crash."

The notice reported: "Victory has designed a Rear Sprocket Cushion Drive Kit that will address this issue under the conditions mentioned above, however, parts are not yet available. Kits are expected to be available in limited quantity beginning the week of December 18, 2006. Repairs will be made by any authorized Victory motorcycle dealer at no cost to you."

The transmission was not drastically re-engineered for the 2002 Freedom engine package, but it was improved and was more reliable going forward than earlier transmissions.

One Polaris insider with awareness of early transmission issues said there were more complaints about transmission noise than there were mechanical breakdowns. "There were very few failures and they were fixed ASAP by Polaris," the source said. "Victory never shimmed inside the case to get the transmission to fit properly. They were always precision components. The basic original transmission design—gear layout, positioning of shafts, etc.—remained the same [even in the original 2002 Freedom package]. There were differences, yes, but it was never completely redesigned from the original. It was a great, robust design from the get-go."

Throughout the brand's history, Victory transmissions remained loud and, to many riders, clunky. The bikes performed well, though, and shifting noise wasn't enough to spoil a great riding experience.

A 1999 V92C had a U.S. MSRP of $12,995. The first-ever Victory model won top cruiser honors from *Cycle World* and *Motorcycle Cruiser* magazines.

This V92C was photographed for the original Victory book at the airport in Osceola, Wisconsin. The airport was across the road from the Polaris engine assembly facility, a large building that was the early home of the Victory Engineering team. A prototype bike was run on the airport's runway as a performance demonstration for the Polaris board of directors. *Lee Klancher*

In an effort to spark sales in the fall of 1999, Victory announced it would offer a limited number of specially equipped units called the V92C SE (Special Edition). Only 400 SE models were scheduled to be produced, in two solid paint colors with gold pinstripes: Solid Candy Antares Red and P.H.A.T. Black. These bikes also had laced wheels (Victory's first), a tiny "Superfly" windshield, and pull-back handlebars.

The V92C got the new Freedom engine starting in model year 2002, and in model year 2003—the final year for the brand's original model—the V92C model name was changed to Classic Cruiser.

The V92C was not a spectacular bike, but it was an historic model as it got Polaris on the road and into the motorcycle business. Without the V92C, Polaris might not be the force it is today in the motorcycle industry with Indian Motorcycle. Model year 2002 and 2003 bikes, with the Freedom engine and transmission, are especially worthwhile investments.

Model Name	V92C	**Front Wheel**	16.0×3.0-inch, five-spoke cast-aluminum wheel
Production Years	1998–2003		
Length	94 inches	**Rear Wheel**	16.0×3.5-inch, five-spoke cast-aluminum wheel
Wheelbase	63.3 inches		
Seat Height	28 inches	**Front Tire**	MT90B/16 Dunlop Elite II MT90
Ground Clearance	5.5 inches	**Rear Tire**	160 80B/16 Dunlop Elite II MT90
Dry Weight	637 pounds	**Frame**	Tubular steel with aluminum sub-frame; uses the engine as a stressed member
Engine	Original Victory Engine		
Exhaust	Staggered dual exhaust		
Final Drive	Belt-drive	**Instrumentation**	Electronic speedometer and tachometer with odometer, resettable tripmeter, fuel gauge, high-beam indicator, oil light, turn signal indicators, low-fuel light, low-voltage light and clock
Fuel Capacity	5 U.S. gallons		
Front Suspension	45mm Marzocchi fork tubes; 5.1 inches of travel		
Front Brakes	Brembo 300mm floating rotor with four-piston caliper		
Rear Suspension	Triangulated swingarm, single Fox shock with spring preload adjustability, 4 inches of travel	**Lights**	Twin-beam headlight, turn signals (front and rear), tail/brake light
		Paint Colors	Antares Red/black and KYSO Blue/black (1998–1999)
Rear Brakes	Brembo 300mm floating rotor with two-piston caliper		

Note: *V92C (called Classic Cruiser in 2003) had the 92-ci Freedom engine for 2002–2003.*

To grasp the brand's design evolution, compare this V92C's ergonomics, which put the rider in a traditional, upright seating position, to those of the Vegas. The lower Vegas seat created a feeling of sitting *in* the bike, rather than *atop* it. Then compare this V92C seating with Victory's ultimate low-slung seating position of the Magnum. *Victory*

This V92C Deluxe has some accessories (horn, grips, tank bag, cargo rack, etc.) but displays stock Deluxe features such as the seat with trim, studded leather saddlebags, passenger backrest, and windshield.

Courtesy Bill Toninato

V92C Deluxe

You could call the 2001 V92C Deluxe the first Victory bagger. Victory answered dealer and rider requests for a bagger by offering a V92C equipped with a windshield, passenger backrest, and studded leather saddlebags, and calling it the V92C Deluxe. The Deluxe seat was trimmed with studs and Conchos. The Deluxe also had 40-spoke laced wheels.

Model Name   V92C Deluxe
Production Years   2001–2002
Note: *Same specs as V92C except Deluxe standard equipment also included a passenger backrest, windshield, leather saddlebags, and studded driver seat.*

High Marks from a Long Test Ride

In 1998, the staff of *Motorcycle Cruiser* magazine rolled up 6,000 miles on Antares Red and Black V92C No. 35. The editors rode the bike from Victory HQ in Minnesota to New York, then across the country to the magazine's offices in Southern California. The bike made a strong first impression.

"The Victory was a perfect partner for exploring the Lincoln Highway. The long, slow days in the saddle—some exceeding fifteen hours—were the ultimate test for a bike's ergonomics. The Victory's seating position and seat weren't merely tolerable, but consistently enjoyable. The stable, firm handling characteristics were appreciated through every twist and turn on the Lincoln. Low-speed predictability was a benefit for backtracking and photo sessions. The bike tracked true at higher speeds as well. I can't tell

you how glad I was to be on it that night in the Alleghenies—just plant it and feed throttle. The wide bar and tires were sweet when the old highway turned to dirt and thick gravel."

The editors wondered if the bike had enough appeal to attract customers, but they were high on its performance.

"If you are looking for a reason not to buy a V92C, we suggest that you decide that you don't like the looks. There is nothing in the way our bike worked that would make us warn you away from it. Yes, the first Victory has a few warts, but none of them are malignant. Perhaps more significantly, none of them are any worse than those on motorcycles from manufacturers who have been building bikes for decades. And this is the first motorcycle model Polaris has ever produced."

V92SC SportCruiser

This was the first of two Victory models that riders and dealers did *not* ask for (also see: Judge). Victory dealers would have liked a bagger or touring bike as the second bike to come out of Spirit Lake, but they got the SportCruiser (SC) instead. This bike did not sell well, yet the majority of SC owners loved the bike and felt it was the better of the first two Victory models. Unfortunately, those loyal owners were limited in number, and the bike was only in production for the 2000 and 2001 model years.

The SC was presented as a heavyweight cruiser with enough sport bike DNA to make it easy for sport bike riders to convert to riding a cruiser. The SportCruiser had the same frame and engine as the V92C, but these features (front to back) were unique to the SC:

- 17-inch rims (1 inch taller than V92C wheels) with sporty Dunlop tires
- Dual 300mm Brembo floating disc front brakes with four-piston calipers (single disc up front on the V92C)
- Low-profile bobbed fenders, front and rear (the first Victory components styled by Industrial Designer Mike Song)

- 50mm-diameter (2 inches) Marzocchi forks (5mm larger than the V92C's)
- Flat track handlebars
- Wrinkle black finish on the engine
- Footpegs instead of floorboards for the driver; the lower controls were set rearward for a sportier feel
- One-piece two-up seat
- Two-into-one exhaust that angled up diagonally across the rear wheel
- Smaller, model-specific, crescent-shaped taillight to fit on the shorter rear fender

The SportCruiser succeeded in delivering a sportier ride than the V92C because the stout SC forks provided front-end strength and minimal flex. Jeff Stone, reviewing the bike for *Men & Motors*, called the forks "something a scaffolder would be proud of!"

Also enhancing performance was the two-into-one exhaust, which was more free-flowing than the stock setup, so the engine produced about 7 hp more than the V92C engine. (Many magazines at the time cited a 10-hp advantage for the V92SC, but Victory was the source of the 7-hp difference.)

This highly stylized action shot from the 2000 Victory brochure shows the new V92SC at speed as well as the size of the original Victory oil cooler, which is mounted at the front of the frame. With the 2002 introduction of the new Freedom, the oil cooler shrunk significantly. *Victory*

The bike's ergonomics also made for a sportier riding experience. The rider's feet were set back rather than stretched forward as on the V92C; there were only pegs for the feet, not floorboards; and the handlebars (called "flat track" bars by Victory), stretched almost straight across rather than bending back to the rider, so a rider might be pulled forward and be more engaged with the bike.

It was a sporty experience despite the fact the SC had one of the tallest seat heights of any Victory ever at 28.5 inches (same as the V92C seat height and 0.2-inch taller than the V92TC, the Touring Cruiser).

Despite its modest sales success, the bike could impress a rider. In a May 2000 review in *Minnesota Motorcycle Monthly*, Sev Pearman noted he was not a fan of cruisers, but the SportCruiser appealed to him:

"I liked the seating position and bar placement. With footpegs instead of 'look-at-me-with-my-extra-weight' floorboards, my thirty-two-inch inseam legs were never cramped. The bars came back putting me in a position just a little forward of a standard bike's 'sit-up-and-beg'

ergonomics. This layout, coupled with an exceptionally comfortable seat (Hooray!) found me squirm-free up until the end of our test ride...

"It rocks. Those fifty-millimeter fork tubes cannot be bent, flexed or made to squirm, even during hard stops. It rails around corners, yet is supple on the superslab. Some bikes fear the chunky abused pavement of MMM's proving grounds, but that is why we bring them there. Not the Victory. It ate up repeated bumpy, peg-scraping corners (Yee-hah!) and remained calm and cool. What a pleasure to ride a bike that actually lives up to its hype.

"The brakes are equally impressive. Victory obviously went 'ka-ching' on the engineering here. Two fingers are more than enough to haul you down smoothly. The lever feel is truly progressive, as well. Squeeze harder, stop sooner. This a level of braking capability better than that of some sport bikes; not to mention light-years ahead of the competition. We could not get them to fade, even with repeated hard stops hauling down my one-eighth of a ton."

A Forking Impressive Intro

Darcy Betlach was the second Victory marketing manager, a position she held as the SC was introduced in 1999. The bike made its private debut at that summer's annual Polaris national sales meeting for dealers, and it was introduced to the public at the Sturgis rally. Motorcycle media were invited to the inside pool area at what was then the Sturgis Best Western hotel near I-90 Exit 32, for the unveiling.

Betlach asked this book's author to write invitation copy that focused on the bike's 50mm forks. But she didn't want technical copy, she wanted edgy copy that used "fork" in place of another "F" word. The invite urged editors with language such as, "Don't fork up and miss this forking huge event," and "Where the fork else would you be?" and "If you're not coming, fork off!"

A Polaris executive saw the copy and told Betlach, "You can't send this out," and her

response was along the lines of, "Too bad, already did."

The lively press intro featured a gospel choir and NASCAR driver Kyle Petty.

Betlach got the SC in front of race fans and potential sport bike riders in 2000, when a Speed Yellow with White Racing Stripes SC was the official sighting bike for the AMA's superbike race series. A race official would ride a lap of the course on the SC prior to each round of racing to ensure the track was ready.

In 2001, Victory offered accessory adhesive-backed graphics for the bike's tank, side covers, and fenders. The graphics featured a styled checkered-flag treatment, except on the side covers, which consisted of the model name.

The P.H.A.T. Black 2000 model had a U.S. MSRP of $13,999, and Champion Red or Steel Grey models cost $14,299.

While the V92C had a single front brake rotor, the SportCruiser had dual discs up front. Impressively, Victory originally used Brembo brakes. This view shows the set-back lower controls, a contrast to the V92C controls, which were mounted close to where the frame tube bent upward in the front. *Victory*

Model Name	V92SC/SportCruiser	**Front Wheel**	17.0×3.5-inch, five-spoke cast-aluminum wheel
Production Years	2000–2001		
Length	90.2 inches	**Rear Wheel**	17.0×5.5-inch, five-spoke cast-aluminum wheel
Wheelbase	63.6 inches		
Seat Height	28.5 inches	**Front Tire**	Dunlop D205F, 120 70B/17
Ground Clearance	5.5 inches	**Rear Tire**	Dunlop D205F, 180 55B/17
Dry Weight	657 pounds	**Frame**	Tubular steel with aluminum sub-frame; uses the engine as a stressed member
Engine	Original Victory Engine		
Exhaust	Two-into-one oversized canister		
Final Drive	Belt-drive	**Instrumentation**	Electronic speedometer and tachometer with odometer, resettable tripmeter, fuel gauge, high-beam indicator, oil light, turn signal indicators, low-fuel light, low-voltage light and clock
Fuel Capacity	5 U.S. gallons		
Front Suspension	50mm Marzocchi fork tubes; 5.1 inches of travel		
Front Brakes	Brembo dual 300mm floating rotors with four-piston caliper		
Rear Suspension	Triangulated swingarm, single Fox gas shock with spring preload adjustability, 4.5 inches of travel	**Lights**	Twin-beam headlight, turn signals (front and rear), tail/brake light
		Paint Colors	P.H.A.T. Black, Steel Grey, Champion Red (2000)
Rear Brakes	Brembo 300mm floating rotor with two-piston caliper		

V92TC, the Touring Cruiser

Victory had loads of news for model year 2002, starting with a new engine, the Freedom V-Twin, about which the company claimed: "Up to 25% more power, 10% better fuel consumption, 100% better looking."

The Freedom engine had the same displacement (92 ci, or 1507cc) and same bore and stroke (97×102mm) as the brand's original engine, but marketing materials noted "virtually everything else has changed." The new engine's compression was increased to 9.2:1 (from 8.5:1), it had redesigned combustion chambers and inlet/exhaust ports, and new camshaft profiles. The largely new Victory engineering team redesigned the cylinders to achieve more cooling by airflow, which allowed them to reduce the oil-cooling effort. Starting in 2002, bikes had smaller oil coolers and a smaller oil pump, which produced a claimed horsepower increase of 2.5 hp.

Victory reported that the new Freedom engine produced 80 hp at the crankshaft and 68 hp when measured at the rear wheel. The peak torque at the crankshaft was 93 foot-pound, and at the rear wheel it measured 77 foot-pound.

A new torque compensator was better at absorbing low-rpm firing impulses (which enhanced low-speed drivability), and a new charging system made it possible to use more powered accessories. The engine also had a new engine control unit (ECU) from Visteon. It offered better performance than the previous unit and was easier to program when accessories such as Stage 1 exhaust were added. The Visteon ECU could be reprogrammed by a software download, while the original unit required a chip replacement.

Additionally, the engine was more smartly styled than the original Victory engine; it was less boxy and more sculpted, with a tapering inward on the lower section of the cylinders.

Cycle World Road Test Editor Don Canet wrote: "The major improvement [for 2002] is in the engine, and especially the drivetrain. It shifts better, it's very smooth, and there's very little drive lash."

Also new for 2002 was the V92TC, the Touring Cruiser. This was Victory's second true bagger (after the V92C Deluxe), and its first touring model. It had a large two-up touring seat; tall windshield; highway

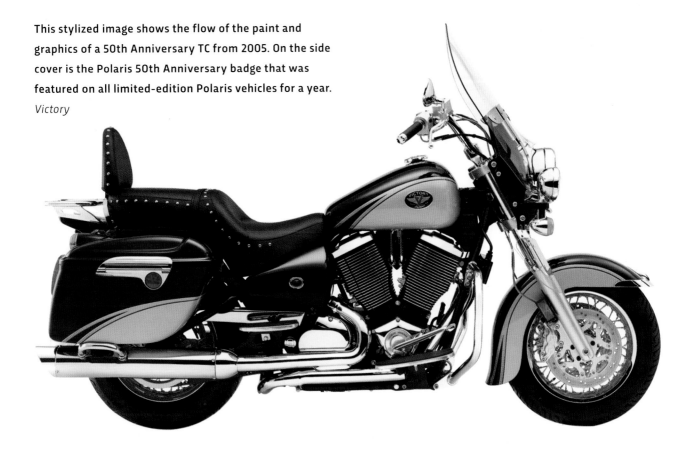

This stylized image shows the flow of the paint and graphics of a 50th Anniversary TC from 2005. On the side cover is the Polaris 50th Anniversary badge that was featured on all limited-edition Polaris vehicles for a year.
Victory

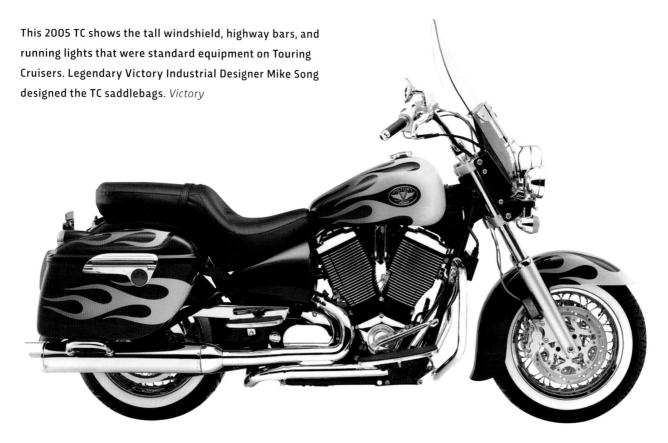

This 2005 TC shows the tall windshield, highway bars, and running lights that were standard equipment on Touring Cruisers. Legendary Victory Industrial Designer Mike Song designed the TC saddlebags. *Victory*

bars; driving lights; floorboards (not pegs) for both the driver and passenger; dual front disc brakes; and most important, large, lockable, and stylish hard saddlebags.

The 2002 V92TC's U.S. MSRP was $14,999 (black) and $15,599 for the two-tones.

The TC could feel large and, at low speeds, top heavy, yet it was not drastically different from the V92C. The TC had a slightly longer wheelbase (65.5 inches versus 63.3 inches), and the same 28.3-inch seat height as the V92C. But the windshield and saddlebags (especially when loaded) added elevated weight, and a full five-gallon fuel tank increased the top-heavy feeling.

Once the bike was rolling, though, it was a Victory, meaning its handling was smooth, easy, intuitive. The dual Brembo front disc brakes did a great job, and the new engine had ample power to haul two-up touring riders. It was also roomy for both driver and passenger, so the TC was a popular choice among tall riders. The bike's bodywork lent itself to two-tone paint, so Victory's Graphic Designer Steve Leszinski created some gorgeous TC paint schemes.

The TC was in the Victory lineup through model year 2006 with minimal changes over the years. In 2007, the Kingpin Tour, a more cost-effective model to produce since it shared numerous components with other models, replaced the TC.

Touring Cruiser Deluxe

Available for model year 2002, the year the TC was introduced, the V92TC Deluxe was essentially an accessorized version of the base model. Standard equipment on the Deluxe included: laced wheels, passenger backrest, fork-mounted wind deflectors, and chrome fender tips. A solid black 2002 V92TC Deluxe had a U.S. MSRP of $15,599. It was also available in four two-tone paint schemes, three of which—Solar Red, Sonic Blue, and Black—were complemented by Vogue Silver. There was also a Champagne and Pearl White color combo. After model year 2003, the V92TC Deluxe was only available when ordered through the Victory Custom Order Program (COP).

Touring Cruiser Deluxe models had enhanced standard equipment, including the rear cargo rack, passenger backrest, and studded seat. *Victory*

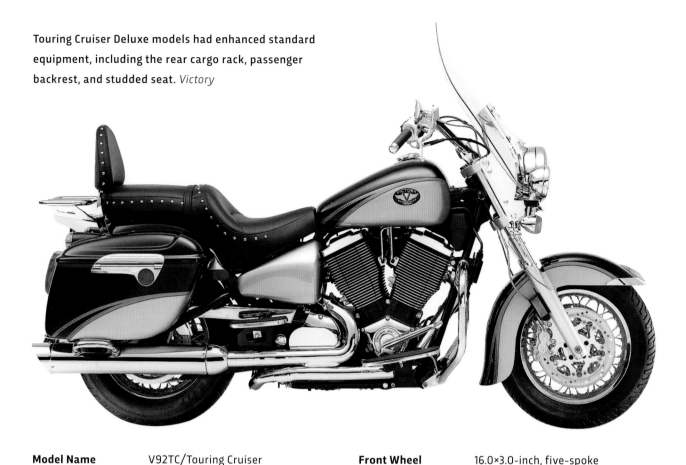

Model Name	V92TC/Touring Cruiser
Production Years	2002–2006
Length	98 inches
Wheelbase	65.5 inches
Seat Height	28.25 inches
Ground Clearance	5.0 inches
Dry Weight	720 pounds
Engine	Victory 92-ci Freedom Engine
Exhaust	Crossover dual exhaust; changeable tips
Final Drive	Belt-drive
Fuel Capacity	5 U.S. gallons
Front Suspension	45mm fork tubes; 5.1 inches of travel
Front Brakes	Dual 300mm floating rotors with four-piston caliper
Rear Suspension	Triangulated swingarm, single gas shock with spring preload adjustability, 4 inches of travel
Rear Brakes	300mm floating rotor with two-piston caliper

Front Wheel	16.0×3.0-inch, five-spoke cast-aluminum wheel
Rear Wheel	16.0×3.5-inch, five-spoke cast-aluminum wheel
Front Tire	MT90B/16 Dunlop 491 Elite II
Rear Tire	160 80B/16 Dunlop D417
Frame	Tubular steel with aluminum sub-frame; uses the engine as a stressed member
Instrumentation	Electronic speedometer and tachometer with odometer, resettable tripmeter, fuel gauge, high-beam indicator, oil light, turn signal indicators, low-fuel light, low-voltage light and clock
Lights	Twin-beam headlight, turn signals (front and rear), tail/brake light
Paint Colors	See Appendix C: V92TC Deluxe

Polaris 50th Anniversary Edition V92TC

Like the 2005 Vegas and Kingpin, the Touring Cruiser was available as a limited-edition Polaris 50th Anniversary Edition. It had a two-tone paint job of Sonic Blue and Vogue Silver with gold pinstriping and a Polaris 50th Anniversary logo on the side cover.

Model Name	Polaris 50th Anniversary Edition V92TC
Production Years	2005
Paint Colors	Sonic Blue and Vogue Silver with gold accents

CHAPTER 4

The Vegas

Introduced in July 2002 as a new 2003 model, the Victory Vegas was monumental. It was, and is: The Bike That Saved the Brand.

By 2001, Victory's early momentum was gone: the V92C was selling modestly; the V92SC (Sport Cruiser) was done; and the V92TC, the Touring Cruiser introduced for model year 2002, lagged in the touring bike market.

Clearly, Victory was not going to win by competing in the classic, retro-styled cruiser world. In light of this, Victory sought to establish a unique identity with a heavyweight American cruiser with sleek, modern style: The Victory Vegas.

It used the Freedom engine that had been introduced in the 2002 models, but otherwise bore no resemblance to earlier Victory models, save for the tank badge. The Vegas looked long and low, with clean, flowing lines, integrated components, and distinctive styling touches. Its signature styling cue was the raised spine that ran the length of both fenders and the fuel tank, tying together the bodywork from end to end.

Along with the raised center spine, the fuel tank had scalloped sides, the first flush-mounted fuel cap on a Victory tank, and a split-tail design that hosted the pointed front end of the driver seat. The fuel cap and tank-seat meeting point featured integration, as did the flush-mounted taillight.

Modern, Custom, Integrated

Mike Song, now the senior staff industrial designer for the Polaris industrial design (ID) department, designed the bike. The bikes Victory was producing pre-Vegas, he said, were "a bit of an issue, they didn't really fit the brand language. We called ourselves 'The New American Motorcycle,' but had dated-looking bikes: plain, not ornate, really nothing. That was the start of my thinking of what Victory should be: more integrated, with a more modern flavor. If we're calling ourselves modern, then the product should embody it."

To Song, bikes featuring integrated styling (not components simply bolted onto bikes in obvious fashion) would portray "modern and custom."

"We wanted something modern, integrated, something that flows a little bit better," he said. "Harley components didn't flow. They were just added onto the bikes. To me, coming from the automotive industry, integrated styling should be visually obvious. The side scallops [of the Vegas fuel tank] were one of

A 2003 Victory Vegas was posed near the famous Las Vegas sign to create the iconic photo that launched "The Bike That Saved the Brand." The image was featured in ads and was widely distributed as a large poster that folded up to become the original Vegas brochure. *Victory*

those design elements. 'Why not put it in the form, not just as graphics added onto the tank?'"

Song spent two or three months styling the bike out of a large block of foam and Bondo. It was a given that the Vegas would use the Freedom engine, but beyond that, Song had tremendous design leeway.

"The original plan was to use the original V92C chassis, but they realized they couldn't get the proportion and the look we wanted," he said. "Compared to what we have now, it was a simple bike. It was a manufacturing challenge, but it didn't seem like it was a struggle. The new engineering team was so pumped and ready to go, there wasn't much resistance at all to what we were creating."

There was a challenge, however, in manufacturing the unique fuel tank. "The center spine had never been done before, so we had to go to Germany for a supplier who could actually do it," Song said. "Eventually, we found a lower-cost supplier."

The Vegas was the Victory division's opportunity to truly forge a brand image. "The project name was CC—Custom Cruiser," Song said. "The project's goal was to reestablish the Victory identity. It was essentially a relaunch of the Victory brand."

It was a misinformed urban legend that the Vegas taillight was the Arlen Ness logo, and that Arlen designed the bike. "No, I designed the taillight. Actually, I have a patent for it," Song said. It's one of four patents he was awarded for the Vegas.

Strutting with Style

The Vegas strutted down the street with a stylish 21-inch front wheel. Yes, it was a front end like that of the Harley-Davidson Softail Deuce, which also had a 21-inch front wheel. But from the triple trees back, the Vegas and Deuce were clearly from different design eras.

The Vegas presented a long, low "Custom Cruiser" look. Yet, it was barely longer than the V92C. The Vegas length and wheelbase were 96 inches and 66.3 inches, respectively, compared to 94 and 63.3 for the V92C.

The seat heights were distinctly different, with the V92C seat at 28 inches and the original Vegas saddle just 26.5 inches from the ground. This made the Vegas popular with shorter and inseam-challenged riders; it would have closed even more sales if the split-tail tank hadn't pushed some riders' legs out

This Vegas fuel tank shows off the model's unique custom design elements. Atop the tank is the raised spine that also ran the length of the front and rear fenders, and the sides are scalloped to host the tank badge. The split tail integrated with the front of the driver seat to create a smooth, custom-look style. *Victory*

A Victory Vegas can haul the mail. This 2005 Vegas, shown with no passenger seat, leans into a rural Wisconsin turn. This bike is loaded with chrome and has a silver engine and frame. *Brian J. Nelson*

rather than letting them extend directly downward for an easy reach to the ground. (The Vegas seat height was lowered to 25.2 inches starting with the Vegas Low in 2008.)

The Vegas was a success from the start. It won awards from several leading motorcycle magazines and attracted attention because of its unique and, to many, appealing styling. And it was a great ride. It was the first instance of Victory engineers providing riders with easy, intuitive, neutral handling, no matter what the makeup of the front end was. (The Magnum was another great example, as it had a taller front wheel and different steering geometry than the stock Cross Country, yet it handled practically identically to that base model.)

The standard Vegas was originally equipped for two-up riding (the Low was a solo-seater), and a large collection of accessories were available to customize its rider comfort, cargo capabilities, and style. The Vegas was a popular canvas for customizers, as its look could be personalized with as little as custom paint, and a custom front wheel changed its look dramatically, too.

Remarkably, while the Vegas 8-Ball remained in the lineup through the brand's final model year (2017), the standard Vegas was discontinued in model years 2013–2015. The standard model returned in model years 2016 and 2017 with the bike available both years in just one color, Sunset Red, with the frame painted to match the bodywork. To Vegas fans, it was a bike that could have stayed in production permanently.

The 2003 Vegas (solid black) had a U.S. MSRP of $14,999. Five years later, a 2008 Vegas listed for

$15,999. In its final year of production, a 2017 Vegas listed for $13,999.

The Vegas changed very little over the years except for its drivetrain, wheels, and paint. Originally powered by the 92-ci Freedom engine with a five-speed transmission, it got the Freedom 100/6 (100 ci, six-speed transmission) starting with model year 2006. Beginning with model year 2011, Vegas models used the Freedom 106/6 package (106 ci with six-speed transmission). Other versions of the Vegas over the years included the Vegas 8-Ball, Vegas 50th Anniversary model, Vegas Low, Ness Signature Series, and Vegas LE.

This 2005 Flame Yellow Vegas was on display at the Barber Vintage Motorsports Museum in Birmingham, Alabama. Along with black frames, Victory also painted them silver in select years, including 2005, which coordinated nicely with the all-silver engine. *Author*

In 2017, Victory's final model year, the Vegas came only with this Sunset Red bodywork, color-matched frame, solo rider setup, new-generation EFI and ignition covers, and the dated round headlight nacelle. *Victory*

Vegas

Model Name	Victory Vegas
Production Years	2003–2012; 2016–2017
Length	96.3 inches
Wheelbase	66.5 inches
Seat Height	26.5 inches
Ground Clearance	5.8 inches
Dry Weight	615 pounds
Engine	Victory 92-ci Freedom Engine
Exhaust	Staggered slash-cut dual exhaust with common volume
Final Drive	Belt-drive
Fuel Capacity	4.5 U.S. gallons
Front Suspension	43mm fork tubes; 5.1 inches of travel
Front Brakes	Brembo 300mm floating rotor with four-piston caliper
Rear Suspension	Triangulated swingarm, single shock with spring preload adjustability, 3.9 inches of travel
Rear Brakes	Brembo 300mm floating rotor with two-piston caliper
Front Wheel	21.0×2.15-inch, 40-spoke laced aluminum wheel
Rear Wheel	18.0×4.5-inch, 40-spoke laced aluminum wheel
Front Tire	80 90/21 Dunlop Cruisemax
Rear Tire	170 60VB/18 Dunlop K591 Elite SP
Frame	Tubular steel; uses the engine as a stressed member
Instrumentation	Electronic speedometer with odometer, resettable tripmeter, high-beam indicator, oil light, turn signal indicators, low-fuel light, and low-voltage light
Lights	Twin-beam headlight, turn signals (front and rear), tail/brake light
Paint Colors	See Appendix C: Vegas

Note: *The Vegas had the 100-ci Freedom engine starting in model year 2006, and the 106-ci Freedom engine starting in model year 2011.*

Vegas 8-Ball

The Vegas 8-Ball debuted in model year 2005. It was Victory's highly effective style and value play: 8-Ball models were available only as all-black bikes, and they typically had features deleted to drop the MSRP below that of the standard base model.

Vegas 8-Ball models had no passenger seat or pegs, and while all other Victory models got six-speed transmissions starting with model year 2006, Vegas 8-Balls had only five-speeds through the 2010 model year. The 8-Ball also retained its "old," original headlight style through the 2010 model year before being upgraded to the more stylish cruiser headlight in 2011. In the early years, the bike had a decal on the front fender of a billiards 8 ball.

Once purchased, no cruiser ever remained completely stock, and the full complement of Vegas accessories fit on the 8-Ball. Interestingly, no 8-Ball model could be called "gloss black" or "matte black." The finish varied from component to component, and you could find three, even four different black coating treatments on a single bike, from wrinkle to matte to gloss.

The Vegas 8-Ball started at $12,999 (2005 U.S. MSRP), went down to $12,499 in 2012, and ended its run at $12,999 (2017).

Model Name	Vegas 8-Ball
Production Years	2005–2017
Paint Colors	Black

Here is a heavily retouched studio shot of a 2005 Vegas 8-Ball, a model that had no accommodations for a passenger and only a five-speed transmission. On the front fender is the decal of the black billiard 8-ball.

Victory

Polaris 50th Anniversary Edition

Victory's model year 2005 lineup was introduced at the Polaris international sales meeting in July 2004, when the company celebrated its 50th anniversary. Selected vehicles from every Polaris division were available as limited-edition 50th Anniversary models, including the Vegas. The bike came in a gorgeous two-tone paint scheme that combined Sonic Blue and Vogue Silver with gold pinstriping. The bike also had a Polaris 50th Anniversary logo on the side cover.

Model Name   Polaris 50th Anniversary
                    Edition Vegas
Production Years 2005
Paint Colors   Sonic Blue and Vogue Silver with
                    gold accents

When Polaris celebrated its 50th anniversary in 2004, every product line featured 50th Anniversary models, including this 2005 Vegas. Each anniversary model had similar Sonic Blue/Vogue Silver paint with gold accents, along with the Polaris 50th badges on this bike's side covers. *Victory*

Vegas Low

In model years 2008 and 2009, Victory offered a Vegas and a Vegas Low, the latter equipped with 2-inch pullback handlebars, lower controls set back 2.25 inches closer to the rider, and a lower seat height of 25.2 inches. Starting with model year 2010, the Vegas Low was gone, and the Vegas assumed the Low's lowered, reduced-reach ergonomics.

Model Name   Vegas Low
Production Years 2008–2009
Paint Colors   See Appendix C: Vegas Low

In production for two model years (a 2009 model is pictured), the Vegas Low had reduced-reach ergonomics. The seat height was lower than that of the standard Vegas, all controls were closer to the driver, and there was no passenger seating. *Victory*

Ness Signature Series Models

The Vegas was the base bike for the 2004 Arlen Ness Signature Series and 2005 Cory Ness Signature Series models. In each case, the master builder loaded the bike with Victory accessories and created a custom paint scheme. A facsimile of the stylist's signature was applied to the side covers, and each bike had a numbered plate to note the bike's limited-edition status. Zach Ness used a Vegas for his Signature Series models in 2011 and 2012.

Model Name	Ness Signature Series Vegas
Production Years	2004–2005; 2011–2012
Paint Colors	See Appendix C: Ness Signature Series Models

The 2004 Arlen Ness Signature Series Vegas was the first Ness special. It featured a paint job designed by Arlen, numerous Ness accessories, a graphic of Arlen's signature on the side covers, and a numbered plate indicating it was a limited edition. *Victory*

Vegas LE

In early 2010, Victory announced the availability of the Vegas LE, a limited-edition model (it was announced that 100 units would be built, but only 30 were) with custom paint and the 106-ci Freedom engine. It was a signal that the model year 2011 Vegas—and every other Victory model—would step up to this bigger engine. The LE model generated little demand; riders were apparently content with the 100-ci engine until the mid-year model changeover.

Model Name	Vegas LE
Production Years	2010
Paint Colors	See Appendix C: Vegas LE

In early 2010, Victory introduced the limited edition Vegas LE with the larger displacement 106/6 Freedom V-Twin, a step up from the 100-ci engine in other 2010 Vegas models. Very few LE models were produced, and this one, No. 1 in the production run, was used as a corporate demo bike. *Author*

CHAPTER 5

The Cruisers

The Victory Vegas was a game changer. The brand could not—and would not—revert to producing retro-styled models like the V92C. (Despite its old-school influences, the High-Ball featured modern styling touches.) Victory was going to rise or fall with progressive, modern styling and outstanding performance.

The V92C was sold through model year 2003, and was known as the Classic Cruiser in that final year. After that, old-school styling largely disappeared, and the Kingpin, with its long-and-low style and flowing fenders followed in the Vegas's tracks.

Picture a Victory dealership showroom where the 2003 models were on display. There would have been a retro (read: old-school) Classic Cruiser parked alongside the sleek, stylish Vegas with its integrated features creating long, flowing lines from end to end. Oh, and on the other side of the Vegas could be a Touring Cruiser with its comparatively bulbous bodywork, whitewalls and laced wheels, and Song-styled saddlebags evoking images of '50s American cars. Two of those models were not long for the lineup, but the Vegas was just beginning a remarkable chapter of modern motorcycle history.

This chapter covers Victory cruisers introduced after the Vegas.

Kingpin

After Mark Blackwell joined Victory as its general manager in 2000, he pledged that the brand would introduce at least one new model every year. The 2004 Kingpin could be viewed as the third such bike, and the second (after the Vegas) to establish Victory as an American cruiser brand that embraced progressive style rather than clinging to a retro look.

The cover of the 2004 Victory brochure carried the headline, "Accelerating the Art of the American Cruiser," which complemented the brand's then-tagline: The New American Motorcycle. The Kingpin was introduced with the headline, "Guts Never Looked So Pretty."

The Kingpin was a fantastic bike. From the triple trees back, it was nearly identical to the Vegas, which made sense. The Vegas was an outstanding platform and was versatile enough to carry another winning model.

Victory redefined "custom cruiser" with the 2006 introduction of the Vegas Jackpot (in later years, called simply the Jackpot). It had a color-matched frame, chrome everywhere possible, a stylish new headlight bezel, 250mm rear tire, and incredible factory paint.
Brian J. Nelson

The biggest mechanical differences between the models were up front, where the Kingpin used Victory's first inverted forks and the 18-inch front wheel matched the rear. (The Vegas had a 21-inch front wheel and an 18-incher in the rear.) This front-end setup gave the Kingpin an extremely stable, confidence-inspiring ride, with no flex (even when the bike was loaded with a passenger and cargo), and more meat on the road than the narrow Vegas tire.

The Kingpin's style signature was its long, flowing fenders. It had a split-tail fuel tank like the Vegas, but Kingpin bodywork did not have the raised spine unique to the Vegas.

Mike Song, now senior staff industrial designer, styled the Kingpin. "I thought the fenders should have a little more drama, that they should flow out of the bike rather than be tucked under it," he recalled.

Positioned as a long-riding cruiser, the Kingpin had floorboards for the driver (and pegs for the passenger), and was commonly shown with accessories such as a windshield, fork-mounted wind deflectors, saddlebags, and a passenger backrest. A large collection of Kingpin accessories was available from day one since numerous Vegas accessories fit on the Kingpin.

In 2005 and 2006, Victory offered the Kingpin Deluxe, which came with a windshield, saddlebags, and a passenger backrest and floorboards (rather than pegs). Starting in model year 2007, the Kingpin was sold with a full complement of touring equipment—including a new trunk—as the Kingpin Tour.

V-Twin Magazine named the 2004 Kingpin "Bike of the Year," and *Motorcyclist Online* noted that its staff had loved the 2003 Vegas, but had even higher praise for the 2004 Kingpin:

"[The Kingpin] actually works better on the road than the Vegas... This isn't to say the Kingpin is a replacement for the strong-selling Vegas. The Kingpin is instead an alternative take on the Vegas concept, reworked with a few choice chassis and styling mods to move Victory beyond the 'custom-cruiser' niche the Vegas occupies and into the more traditional, 'fat-fendered' category... The fact that the Kingpin actually works better on the road than the Vegas is but a happy coincidence.

"The Kingpin's inverted fork features cartridge internals (a first for Victory) and, as a result, the separate compression and rebound damping circuits are very well balanced. The improvement is especially

The Kingpin was an evolved variation of the Vegas. The bikes were nearly identical from the triple trees back, but had distinctly different front ends. The stable and planted Kingpin front had inverted forks and an 18-inch front wheel with a 130mm-wide tire. The stylish Vegas end had a 21-inch wheel and 90mm-wide tire. *Victory*

Kevin Cross had a beautifully customized Kingpin with custom-painted Corbin bags, several custom accessories, and a raked front end. Have no doubt the engine and exhaust were modified to unleash impressive power. Cross was the service manager of a Florida Polaris dealership for many years and was known online as KevinX, the ultimate answer man for Victory tech questions. He now owns and operates Southern MotorwoRx in High Springs, Florida. *Author*

apparent at low speeds. On tight, big-bumped bits (Trinity Road, for those of you familiar with Sonoma County) the Kingpin does a stellar job of keeping the tires on the tarmac. Only at higher speeds (the open sweepers on Butts Canyon and Pope Valley Roads back in Napa) can you induce any wallow, indicating a slightly undersprung/underdamped rear shock. The upshot is that the rear end is spine-savingly soft at sane speeds, which is what most cruiser riders want."

Starting with model year 2006, the Kingpin used the Freedom 100/6 (a 100-ci engine mated with a six-speed transmission): the powerplant introduced in the 2005 Hammer. In model year 2011, the Kingpin got the ultimate Victory powerplant, the Freedom 106/6 V-Twin, a 106-ci engine with a six-speed transmission.

With the introduction of the Cross-bike platform in 2010, bikes like the Cross Country replaced the Kingpin as the brand's versatility leader. And the High-Ball, introduced in January 2011, represented the new-generation Victory cruiser platform, thus phasing out the Kingpin. The venerable cruiser was available in only two colors for 2011, and one of those, two-tone Vogue Silver and White, was the lone Kingpin paint scheme available in the bike's final year, 2012.

The black 2004 Kingpin U.S. MSRP was $14,999, and rose to $15,299 for 2005.

The Kingpin was almost as stylish as the Vegas and had similar bodywork. Its flowing fenders provided large canvases for color or graphics. This 2007 Kingpin has Boardwalk Blue and Pearl White paint. *Victory*

Model Name	Kingpin	**Front Wheel**	18.0×3.0-inch, six-spoke cast-aluminum wheel
Production Years	2004–2012	**Rear Wheel**	18.0×5.0-inch, six-spoke cast-aluminum wheel
Length	99.1 inches		
Wheelbase	66.5 inches	**Front Tire**	130 70-18 Dunlop Elite II
Seat Height	26.5 inches	**Rear Tire**	180 55-B18 Dunlop D417
Ground Clearance	5.8 inches	**Frame**	Tubular steel; uses the engine as a stressed member
Dry Weight	639 pounds		
Engine	Victory 92-ci Freedom Engine	**Instrumentation**	Electronic speedometer with odometer, resettable tripmeter, high-beam indicator, oil light, turn signal indicators, low-fuel light, and low-voltage light
Exhaust	Staggered slash-cut dual exhaust with common volume		
Final Drive	Belt-drive		
Fuel Capacity	4.5 U.S. gallons		
Front Suspension	Inverted cartridge telescopic 43mm fork	**Lights**	Twin-beam headlight, turn signals (front and rear), tail/brake light
Front Brakes	300mm floating rotor with four-piston caliper	**Paint Colors**	See Appendix C: Kingpin
Rear Suspension	Triangulated swingarm, single shock with spring preload adjustability, 3.9 inches of travel		
Rear Brakes	300mm floating rotor with two-piston caliper		

Note: *The Kingpin had the 100-ci Freedom engine starting in model year 2006, and, starting with model year 2011, the 106-ci Freedom engine.*

Kingpin Deluxe

Available for model years 2005 and 2006, the Deluxe was a precursor to the Kingpin Tour and gave the lineup two baggers (along with the Touring Cruiser). The Kingpin Deluxe came with a windshield, saddlebags, fork-mounted wind deflectors, a passenger backrest, and passenger floorboards instead of pegs. The U.S. MSRP for the 2006 Kingpin Deluxe was $17,499.

Model Name	Kingpin Deluxe
Production Years	2005–2006
Paint Colors	See Appendix C: Kingpin Deluxe

The Kingpin was Victory's most versatile platform until the Cross bikes were developed. This Black over Vogue Silver 2005 Kingpin Deluxe provided the riders with cargo space, enhanced passenger comfort, and the protection of a windshield and fork-mounted air deflectors. *Victory*

Polaris 50th Anniversary Edition Kingpin

Like the 2005 Vegas and Touring Cruiser, the Kingpin was available as a limited-edition Polaris 50th Anniversary Edition. Its two-tone paint job combined Sonic Blue and Vogue Silver with gold pinstriping, and the bike had a Polaris 50th Anniversary logo on the side cover.

As parent company Polaris celebrated its first half-century in business, Victory introduced the 50th Anniversary Kingpin. This 2005 model had Sonic Blue/Vogue Silver paint with gold accents, and Polaris 50th badges on the side covers. *Victory*

Model Name	Polaris 50th Anniversary Edition Kingpin
Production Years	2005
Paint Colors	Sonic Blue and Vogue Silver with gold accents

Kingpin 8-Ball

In model year 2008, Victory gave the Kingpin its blacked-out, no-frills, one-low-price 8-Ball treatment. The Kingpin 8-Ball had minimal chrome, no accommodations for the passenger, and the transmission was a five-speed, not the six-speed of the standard model in 2008–2010. The Kingpin 8-Ball got the Freedom 106/6 with the six-speed for 2011, its final year of production.

Model Name	Kingpin 8-Ball
Production Years	2008–2011
Paint Colors	Black

The Kingpin 8-Ball was a solid value. Most years it "only" had a five-speed transmission. Although it never had passenger accommodations, it was otherwise a standard Kingpin, and a great bike. *Brian J. Nelson*

Kingpin Low

In model year 2009, the Kingpin Low offered riders a lower version of the bike with upper and lower controls repositioned about 2 inches closer to the rider. The Kingpin Low had 5.3 inches of ground clearance (0.5 inch less than standard), and a 25.2-inch seat height (1.3 inches lower). The Low had 2-inch pullback handlebars and the footpegs were set 2.25 inches closer to the rider. Designed to provide a solo rider with a confidence-inspiring ride, the bike had no passenger seat or pegs.

The Kingpin Low was available for just one year, and unlike the standard Vegas—which assumed the Low model's ergonomics starting in model year 2010—the standard Kingpin of model years 2010–2012 retained the original ergo setup.

Model Name	Kingpin Low
Production Years	2009
Paint Colors	See Appendix C: Kingpin Low

Available only in model year 2009, the Kingpin Low gave the driver a lower seat height, reduced reach to the controls, and no passenger seating. The Low setup made more sense on the Vegas with its broader appeal, but the demand wasn't there for the lower Kingpin. *Victory*

Arlen Ness Signature Series Kingpin

The Kingpin was the base bike for the 2005 Arlen Ness Signature Series model, which featured an Arlen-designed paint scheme, loads of accessories, a facsimile of Arlen's signature on the side covers, and a limited-edition numbered plate. It was the only year the Kingpin got the Ness treatment, as the Vegas Jackpot became the Ness canvas of choice for the next several years. The bike's "Purple Haze" paint actually looked maroon, and wasn't all that appealing compared to the beautiful paint of the 2004 Ness Vegas and the stunning 2005 Cory Ness Vegas. One insider story was that, in production, the Ness Kingpin paint did not match the purple shade Arlen had designated when he styled the bike.

Model Name	Arlen Ness Signature Kingpin
Production Years	2005
Paint Colors	"Purple Haze" and black

The 2005 Kingpin was the base model for the second Signature Series bike styled by Arlen Ness. Along with gloss black, it featured an accent color called "Purple Haze." Victory legend is that the production paint wasn't as bright (nor appealing) as the color Arlen originally selected, and the bike had a small production run, enhancing its rare nature. *Victory*

Introduced in 2007, the Kingpin Tour had equipment for two-up touring, but the space for two riders was cramped compared to that of the Vision and the Cross bikes that came later. The "Top Box" load capacity was listed as twenty pounds, but rest assured, riders stuffed way more than twenty pounds of cargo in there. *Brian J. Nelson*

Kingpin Tour

By adding accessories to the smooth-riding Kingpin, Victory had its second-ever touring model, the Kingpin Tour, which was in the lineup from 2007–2009.

Touring equipment that was standard on the Kingpin Tour included the saddlebags, windshield, fork-mounted wind deflectors, passenger floorboards, and the new-in-2007 trunk that included an integrated, padded passenger backrest.

The Kingpin Tour was a comfortable, long-riding bike, but it was a place holder while Victory developed new, more dynamic touring models.

Before the Vision was introduced, the Kingpin was arguably the smoothest-riding Victory, so the Kingpin Tour was a good touring bike, especially for a solo rider. For two-up riders, the seating could be cramped, so trip duration was likely determined by the passenger's comfort.

Unfortunately, the size—especially the vertical depth—of saddlebags for Vegas and Kingpin models was limited because the bikes had stacked dual exhausts on the right side. The Kingpin trunk also was not large, especially compared to those of the Vision and Cross Country Tour. But Victory testing was always thorough and prudent—the trunk on the Kingpin Tour was as large as the engineers determined was safe and accommodated the desired ride quality. The trunk's load capacity was rated by Victory at 20 pounds, but rest assured, consumers commonly stuffed way more than that in the box.

A black 2007 Kingpin had a U.S. MSRP of $15,999, while the Kingpin Tour started at $17,999.

Model Name	Kingpin Tour	**Rear Brakes**	300mm floating rotor with two-piston caliper
Production Years	2007–2009		
Length	102.9 inches	**Front Wheel**	18.0×3.0-inch cast-aluminum wheel
Wheelbase	65.5 inches	**Rear Wheel**	18.0×5.0-inch cast-aluminum wheel
Seat Height	26.5 inches	**Front Tire**	130/70 B18 Dunlop 491 Elite II
Ground Clearance	5.8 inches	**Rear Tire**	180 55-B18 Dunlop D417
Dry Weight	741 pounds	**Frame**	Tubular steel; uses the engine as a stressed member
Engine	Victory 100-ci Freedom Engine		
Exhaust	Staggered slash-cut dual exhaust with common volume	**Instrumentation**	Electronic speedometer with odometer, resettable tripmeter, high-beam indicator, oil light, turn signal indicators, low-fuel light, and low-voltage light
Final Drive	Belt-drive		
Fuel Capacity	4.5 U.S. gallons		
Front Suspension	Inverted cartridge telescopic 43mm fork		
		Lights	Twin-beam headlight, turn signals (front and rear), tail/brake light
Front Brakes	300mm floating rotor with four-piston caliper		
		Paint Colors	See Appendix C: Kingpin Tour
Rear Suspension	Triangulated swingarm, single shock with spring preload adjustability, 3.9 inches of travel		

Hammer

Victory introduced the Hammer as part of the 2005 model lineup and it appealed to sport bike riders far more than the SportCruiser had. Victory said the Hammer established a new category, that of "Muscle Cruiser," and in fact, it had more power than any other Victory at the time.

The 2005 Hammer introduced the Victory Freedom 100/6 V-Twin, a 100-ci V-twin with a six-speed transmission; sixth gear was an overdrive. It was among the largest-displacement engines in a production motorcycle at the time, and Victory claimed it was the first production version of a six-speed transmission.

The engine delivered everything the Freedom engine was becoming known for: good acceleration, smooth power, minimal maintenance, and great reliability. The 100-ci engine was a distinct step up from the original 92-ci Freedom engine that was still used in all other 2005 Victory models. The Hammer also had a sportier, stiffer suspension setup, not the plush, lounge chair suspension common to many cruisers.

Product Manager Gary Laskin wanted this Toxic Green paint with Tribal Tattoo graphics to be polarizing. It wasn't everyone's cup of tea, though proved popular on the 2005 Hammer. After all, people riding this muscle cruiser weren't trying to hide, they wanted to be noticed. *Victory*

There's lots to see on this accessorized 2007 Hammer, such as the bike's 250mm-wide rear tire and "V" handlebar. The stylish headlight nacelle, which was introduced in 2006 on the Jackpot, also appeared on the 2007 Hammer and other Victory cruisers. *Victory*

When you hit the gas on a Hammer, you were firmly planted on the seat and the power transfer was instant and impressive.

Plus, power was being transferred to another of the bike's signature components: a 250mm-wide Dunlop rear tire that was shown off by the high-cut rear fender. Victory engineers worked with Dunlop on the tire and it worked very well. At low speeds, when the bike wasn't leaned over, the rider had to crank the handlebars to get the bike to turn; otherwise, that flat, wide tire would push the bike straight ahead. On the road, though, the bike handled beautifully, and there were no constant reminders of the rear tire's size. At speed, maneuvers such as cornering and lane changes were easy and intuitive.

The rear tire was mounted on an 8.5-inch-wide, 18-inch-tall wheel. Up front was an 18-inch wheel with a 5.08-inch-wide tire, an ideal mate for the rear meat. Like the Kingpin, the Hammer forks were inverted, and the front end was set up stiffer (or, if you like, stronger), like the rear suspension.

To complement the extra power of the bigger engine, the Hammer came with dual front brake discs.

Another signature styling element was the passenger seat cowl. The bike had a one-piece seat with the driver seated in a modestly padded dish and the passenger on a miniscule pad that extended off the back of the driver seat. A plastic cowl, color-matched to the bike's bodywork, snapped into place over the passenger seat. With a solo rider aboard and the cowl in place, the bike looked like it had only a solo seat.

A Victory accessory called the Superfly Windscreen was a small windshield (available in clear or black) with three holes. Those holes aligned with the mounting

With its blacked-out styling, the 2011 Hammer S lived up to the brand's marketing classification of "muscle cruiser." The numerous black components and limited chrome helped the Suede Black and red paint really pop. *Brian J. Nelson*

pegs of the passenger seat cowl, so a rider could remove the cowl and snap it into the Superfly for convenient storage and a unique, color-matched add-on.

Victory introduced the Hammer to the motorcycle media with a press ride in Texas Hill Country. The bike impressed the media, including Aaron Frank, who was then writing for *Motorcyclist* magazine. He wrote: "...the Hammer is undeniably bad-ass... it's impossible to overestimate the visual impact the fat-tire Hammer makes."

Thunder Press Editor-in-Chief Terry Roorda wrote that the bike performed "brilliantly. The Hammer's power is prodigious. It's also linear and predictable, pouring on without a blip or fade from an idle to the top of its power band. It's usable power for the way most of us ride, pulling ferociously in the low revs and hitting its full stride in the passing range between 3,500 and 4,000 rpm."

In 2005, the model's first year on the market, it was available in four solid colors and in two paint schemes with Tribal Tattoo Graphics. One of those colors with graphics was Toxic Green, an outrageously bright green that then-product manager Gary Laskin selected for its polarizing effect. He knew people would love or hate it, and in the end, more loved it.

Victory introduced the 106-ci version of the Freedom engine with the 2008 Vision models, and the Hammer was among the models to get the 106-ci engine starting in 2009.

The Hammer originally came with V-shaped handlebars to conjure the notion, "V for Victory." Some riders loved the custom-look bars, which were broad but extended back toward the rider. Others disliked the steering leverage, especially on a supposedly high-performance bike where control was paramount. Hammer S and Hammer 8-Ball models always had more-traditional buckhorn-style bars, and in 2010 and 2011, the base Hammer also had buckhorn bars.

The Hammer remained in the Victory lineup through model year 2011, then was discontinued. The Hammer S kept the model name in the lineup from 2007–2012, and again in 2016 and 2017; there was no standard Hammer or Hammer S in 2013–2015.

A solid black 2005 Hammer had a U.S. MSRP of $16,499. In 2007, the first Hammer S had a list price of $19,749, while the standard model was $16,899.

Model Name	Hammer
Production Years	2005–2011
Length	92.7 inches
Wheelbase	65.7 inches
Seat Height	26.3 inches
Ground Clearance	5.8 inches
Dry Weight	659 pounds
Engine	Victory 100-ci Freedom Engine
Exhaust	Large-bore slash-cut dual exhaust with common volume
Final Drive	Belt-drive
Fuel Capacity	4.5 U.S. gallons
Front Suspension	Inverted cartridge telescopic forks, 43mm diameter; 5.1 inches of travel
Front Brakes	Dual 300mm floating rotors with four-piston caliper
Rear Suspension	Forged and cast-aluminum swingarm, single shock with spring preload adjustability, 3.9 inches of travel
Rear Brakes	300mm floating rotor with two-piston caliper
Front Wheel	18.0×3.0-inch cast-aluminum wheel
Rear Wheel	18.0×8.5-inch cast-aluminum wheel
Front Tire	130/70R18 Dunlop Elite 3
Rear Tire	250/40R18 Dunlop Elite 3
Frame	Tubular steel; uses the engine as a stressed member
Instrumentation	Electronic speedometer with odometer, resettable tripmeter, high-beam indicator, oil light, turn signal indicators, low-fuel light, and low-voltage light
Lights	Twin-beam headlight, turn signals (front and rear), tail/brake light
Paint Colors	See Appendix C: Hammer

Note: *Hammer models had the 106-ci Freedom engine starting in model year 2009.*

This 2009 Hammer shines with its copious chrome, and no doubt breathes fire with its two-into-one exhaust. Victory's 2009 models came with the monochrome tank badge logo, which the company claimed it would use for an additional 10 years, but a full-color badge returned in 2010. *Lee Klancher*

The 2008 Hammer S effectively evokes the spirit of American muscle cars with its competition stripe running the length of the bike, and the muscle cruiser's dynamic styling. *Victory*

Hammer S

For the first time in 2007, the lineup had two Hammer models: the standard muscle cruiser and the Hammer S (for "Sport"). The S was a limited-edition model with a premium muscle car–inspired paint, several blacked-out features (including the engine), a tachometer alongside the speedo, and custom wheels from Performance Machine (PM). For 2007, the Hammer S had a black-and-red paint scheme and red powder-coated "Gatlin" wheels from PM. It also had the more stylish headlight nacelle that had been introduced on the 2006 Vegas Jackpot, and the name "HAMMER" appeared on both sides of the rear bodywork just under the passenger seat cowl.

Hammer S models usually had two-tone paint schemes, commonly with broad racing stripes. In several years, the headlight nacelle also had two-tone paint. The Hammer S always had buckhorn handlebars, not the "V" bars of the early Hammers.

Instead of chrome, the 2009 Hammer S featured blacked-out features, which complemented the paint scheme and gave the bike a powerful presence. *Victory*

Model Name	Hammer S
Production Years	2007–2012 and 2016–2017
Paint Colors	See Appendix C: Hammer S

Hammer 8-Ball

The beauty of the stock Hammer was that there wasn't much Victory could remove when creating a Hammer 8-Ball. The two-up seat with the cowl over the passenger seat remained in place on the Hammer 8-Ball, but the front braking had only a single rotor, not the popular twin-rotor setup that appealed to Hammer riders. In model year 2010, the Hammer 8-Ball's first year, Victory also removed sixth gear, but all later Hammer 8-Ball models came with the six-speed gearbox.

The Hammer 8-Ball had everything the stock Hammer had: muscle cruiser style, good power, and smooth handling. The Hammer 8-Ball was in the lineup from 2010 to 2015 (and was available only in Europe in model years 2016–2017).

Model Name	Hammer 8-Ball
Production Years	2010–2015
Paint Colors	Black

The Hammer 8-Ball was an outstanding value. In some model years (including the 2010 shown here), sixth gear and one of the dual front brake rotors were not included. But the blacked-out 8-Ball was otherwise equipped just like a standard Hammer. *Victory*

Vegas Jackpot

Many Victory riders won a lot of "Best Custom" trophies after entering bone-stock Vegas Jackpots in shows and contests. The Vegas had been categorized by Victory as a custom cruiser, but *this*, the Vegas Jackpot, *this* was a custom cruiser.

(The model was called the Vegas Jackpot from 2006–2012, and was known as the Jackpot in 2013 and 2014. It was available in a single paint scheme in each of those final two years of production.)

Mechanically, this extreme custom cruiser combined the Hammer's rear end (250mm rear tire) and the Vegas front end (21-inch wheel and narrow tire). The front fender, fuel tank, and driver seat were the same as on the Vegas. To cover the 250mm tire, the rear fender was a wider version of the Vegas fender.

Among the bike's custom-look elements were its stylish headlight nacelle (streamlined, not simply a round bucket like on earlier Victory models); the color-matched frame; the stylish front wheel (almost always polished or billet); and an abundance of chrome, including the rear fender struts, forks, exhaust, belt cover, and more.

Victory motorcycles always had premium paint. An outside vendor had painted the bodywork of the earliest bikes, the V92C and V92SC, but from that point on, paintwork was done in-house at the

Introduced for model year 2006, the Vegas Jackpot made an immediate impact with its custom style. The stock 2006 Jackpot on the right is as eye-catching as the Cory Ness Signature Series model on the left. *Brian J. Nelson*

For many years, the Jackpot was available in solid Gloss Black (right), which was an ideal (and the least expensive) starting point for a rider who planned to add custom paint. The Jackpot was never offered as an 8-Ball. *Victory*

Spirit Lake facility. (In the brand's final two years of production, some paint work was done in Spearfish, South Dakota, after Polaris purchased the former Lehman Trike production plant.)

Victory paint quality was on full display with Vegas Jackpot models. Even solid-colored models dazzled as their pristine finish shone alongside the abundant chrome on the bikes. Graphic Designer Steve Leszinski, of the Polaris industrial design team, created some head-turning graphics for the Vegas Jackpot, some of them outrageous, some with beautiful interpretations on classic flames. The 2011 and 2012 paint options included schemes with a

pinup girl in the style of warbird nose art on the side covers.

The Jackpot's final bow was its most modest appearance. For 2014, the Jackpot was available with only one paint scheme, Sunset Red and Gloss Black, with uninspired (for a Jackpot) tank graphics and less chrome than was traditional on this model. Sadly, the bike had the old, round headlight nacelle for the first time. Fittingly, the glamorous Jackpot was never released as a "Plain Jane" 8-Ball model, though it probably would have sold extremely well, giving customizers a blank canvas for their custom treatments.

Among the paint schemes available for 2007 Jackpots was this Pearl White with Extreme Graphics package. The vivid paint was complemented by copious chrome. *Victory*

The Jackpot was a classic bar-hopper—stylish and stunning when going straight and when parked outside the hot spots—but it was a true Victory, meaning its owners rode the wheels off the bikes. There are several true hard-asses who completed Iron Butt rides on Jackpots. When it made its 2006 debut, it had the Freedom 100/6 package. Starting in 2009, it was powered by the 106/6 package with the 106-ci engine.

It was also a classic example of Victory engineering acumen. If the big rear tire pushed at low speeds on a Hammer, imagine what it could do on a Jackpot with its 90mm-wide tire. Yet Jackpots, like Hammers, handled easily and naturally once the bike was at speed.

The solid black 2006 Vegas Jackpot had a list price of $17,499.

Model Name	Vegas Jackpot
Production Years	2006–2014
Length	96.3 inches
Wheelbase	66.3 inches
Seat Height	25.7 inches
Ground Clearance	5.3 inches
Dry Weight	644 pounds
Engine	Victory 100-ci Freedom Engine
Exhaust	Staggered slash-cut dual exhaust with common volume
Final Drive	Belt-drive
Fuel Capacity	4.5 U.S. gallons
Front Suspension	Conventional telescopic forks, 43mm diameter; 5.1 inches of travel
Front Brakes	300mm floating rotor with four-piston caliper
Rear Suspension	Forged and cast-aluminum swingarm, single shock with spring preload adjustability, 3.0 inches of travel
Rear Brakes	300mm floating rotor with two-piston caliper
Front Wheel	21.0×2.15-inch cast-aluminum wheel
Rear Wheel	18.0×8.55-inch cast-aluminum wheel
Front Tire	80 90/21 Dunlop Cruisemax
Rear Tire	250/40R18 Dunlop Elite 3
Frame	Tubular steel; uses the engine as a stressed member
Instrumentation	Electronic speedometer with odometer, resettable tripmeter, high-beam indicator, oil light, turn signal indicators, low-fuel light, and low-voltage light
Lights	Twin-beam headlight, turn signals (front and rear), tail/brake light
Paint Colors	See Appendix C: Vegas Jackpot

Note: *The Jackpot had the 106-ci Freedom engine starting with model year 2009.*

Ness Signature Series Jackpots

The Vegas Jackpot (and later, the Vision) was probably the best base bike for Arlen and Cory Ness to create their Signature Series specials. In the Jackpot's first year, 2006, both Ness models were based on this model. It was the bike of choice for both of them in 2007 and 2008, too. Cory styled a stunning monochrome Jackpot for his 2009 model, and his 2010 model was the final time the Jackpot was used as a Ness model.

Model Name	Ness Signature Series Jackpots
Production Years	2006–2010
Paint Colors	See Appendix C: Ness Signature Series Models

The Jackpot was an ideal bike for Arlen and Cory Ness to customize into Signature Series models. For 2006, they both styled Jackpots, including this Cory Ness Signature Series Vegas Jackpot. *Victory*

High-Ball

What a bike. What a platform. The High-Ball was introduced in January 2011 in a live webcast from a well-scrubbed pool hall in Manhattan, in conjunction with the International Motorcycle Show taking place at the time in town.

After significant build-up, the High-Ball paid dividends in full, both on first look and especially on the road. It represented the outstanding next generation of Victory cruisers with its bare-bones composition, beautifully balanced platform, and powerful Freedom 106/6 engine. The High-Ball was extremely successful and sold well for several years. (It would later be fitted with standard handlebars and re-ascend as a second model: the Gunner.)

The High-Ball made an immediate visual impact. The ape hanger handlebars were the focal point,

but the bike was also clean, if not Spartan, with its bobbed fenders, matte black finish evoking a rat bike's spray paint treatment, modest (and unique to that point) Victory graphics, and retro laced wheels and whitewall tires.

The High-Ball was a street-legal motorcycle, but its high bars created the image—for rider and onlooker alike—of an outlaw rider. In March 2011, Peter Jones of *Cycle World* conveyed it adroitly, writing:

"Ape hangers aren't just defining of a riding position, they're a statement. Ape hangers are an evil gesture. Ape hangers are a bit like flipping off the world, without having to separate one finger to do so. If there's a picture of you sitting on a High-Ball on your Facebook page, you might want to remove it before

The High-Ball was an outstanding merger of classic bobber style with modern technology. The introduction of this model extended Victory's reputation for outstanding cruisers, and provided the brand with a versatile platform that worked equally well with traditional handlebars. *Victory*

With the handlebar raised, the rider enjoyed a comfortable reach to the bars and full control of the bike. The High-Ball was the most popular Victory at demo rides for at least a year after it was introduced, and it was no doubt the first ape hanger bike many riders ever experienced. *Victory*

applying for a job (depending on the job, of course). So does it matter if these bars are comfortable or not? Probably not. And if you don't regularly ride a bike with ape hangers, the question of their comfort can't be fairly judged."

Since some state laws limited handlebar or upper controls height, the High-Ball was engineered with adjustable handlebars. Near each end of the bar were two sets of *détentes*, which allowed the controls to be positioned for a bars-up rider, or rotated when the bars were set in a lower, pulled-back position.

Cycle World's Jones also expressed why the High-Ball (and later, the Gunner) rode so well:

"Functionally, the High-Ball is defined by those high bars and its pair of matched 16×3.5 -inch wire-spoke wheels. The front tire is a fat 130 while the rear is a fatter 150. This combination makes it one of the better handling bikes in the company's pure-cruiser stable. It turns with neutral ease. Also, despite its 'low' ride, its suspension does a good job eating bumps, from potholes to railroad tracks. It's a kidney-friendly bike. And for those riders who like to drag parts and chance indiscretions, the High-Ball is stable in gnarly, undulating sweepers

ridden through at a mph that equals the bike's count of claimed horsepower, whose number I'm hoping the editor doesn't specifically mention here."

Riding on those meaty tires, the High-Ball was balanced, smooth, easy handling, and fun as hell. Newcomers to apes commonly wondered if they would have to adjust their riding style, their leaning, or low-speed steering, but with the High-Ball, the answer was "no" on all counts. At speed on the road, the bike's handling was fluid, intuitive, and not really different at all from riding a bike with traditional bars. At full lock in a parking lot, yes, a rider could run out of arm reach, but that was a short-term, low-speed situation.

Consider the power, or more specifically, the power-to-weight; the 2013 High-Ball weighed in at 659 pounds (dry), while that year's Vision weighed 869 pounds—and both bikes used the same Freedom 106/6 powerplant.

The original paint scheme, used in model years 2012 and 2013, was fantastic, as were the truly all-black 2015 and 2017 paint jobs. Alternative paint jobs were offered to help denote differences in model years: there was a flamed High-Ball available for 2014, and a Suede Nuclear Sunset Orange version for 2017.

In contrast to the High-Ball's badass black paint schemes, this Suede Nuclear Sunset Orange paint was offered for 2017.
Victory

Throughout its history, the High-Ball was always sold as a solo cruiser with no passenger equipment. But a wide variety of accessories were possible since numerous Vegas accessories also fit on the High-Ball (and Gunner).

What a platform, what a bike. If Victory would have survived with, say, a pared-down, greatest-hits lineup of pure winners, cruisers could have been covered by offering the High-Ball platform and a customer's choice of bars to finish it off as either a High-Ball or Gunner.

The original 2011 High-Ball had a list price of $13,499, which was also the price of the final 2017 black model; the orange 2017 model cost $13,749.

Model Name	High-Ball
Production Years	2011–2017
Length	92.5 inches
Wheelbase	64.8 inches
Seat Height	25.0 inches
Ground Clearance	4.7 inches
Dry Weight	659 pounds
Engine	Victory 106-ci Freedom Engine
Exhaust	Staggered slash-cut dual exhaust with crossover
Final Drive	Belt-drive
Fuel Capacity	4.5 U.S. gallons
Front Suspension	Conventional telescopic forks, 43mm diameter; 5.1 inches of travel
Front Brakes	300mm floating rotor with four-piston caliper
Rear Suspension	Single mono-tube gas shock, cast-aluminum swingarm with rising rate linkage, spring pre-load adjustability, 3.0 inches of travel
Rear Brakes	300mm floating rotor with two-piston caliper
Front Wheel	16.0×3.5-inch laced-aluminum wheel
Rear Wheel	16.0×3.5-inch laced-aluminum wheel
Front Tire	130/90-16 67H Dunlop Cruisemax
Rear Tire	150/80-16 71H Dunlop Cruisemax
Frame	Tubular steel; uses the engine as a stressed member
Instrumentation	Electronic speedometer with odometer, resettable tripmeter, high-beam indicator, oil light, turn signal indicators, low-fuel light, and low-voltage light
Lights	Twin-beam headlight, turn signals (front and rear), tail/brake light
Paint Colors	Black and white with graphics (2011)

Judge

The seed that grew into the Judge was planted with the creation of the Hammer. "When the Hammer was new, I really liked it," said Greg Brew, Polaris director of industrial design. "When it was on target and on trend, it was a bit of a muscle bike. I dug that."

The Hammer represented the powerful, performance-minded image Victory wanted to convey and bring to the streets. But eventually, a wide rear tire became common in the industry, and Brew said at the time, "The 250 rear tire is Wal-Mart. Everyone has it. I'd been squirming around that it was time to do a performance bike."

The vision for that bike (eventually the Judge) was to pick up where the Hammer left off. "We wanted to build a Hammer stripped for fighting weight," Brew said. "The new bike would be more lean, more athletic, much more ready to go in the corner."

He and Senior Industrial Designer Mike Song had to operate within budget constraints that limited how "new" they could make the new bike. If it could borrow from other projects and models, the bean counters would be happy.

Song and Brew turned to a somewhat unlikely source: the brand's most successful model ever.

A Judge, with accessory side cover decals, parked just outside the Spirit Lake city limits in October 2012. The author took the bike on an Iron Cheek ride (500 miles; half an Iron Butt) and loved the ride. This was an original bike, with the relatively straight handlebar and the lower controls set back from where they ended up one year later. *Author*

After poor response to the original Judge ergonomics and styling, Victory made changes for the North American market. The driver position was made virtually identical to that of the Vegas, and the side cover lost its race number styling. *Victory*

"When Mike and I originally wanted to do the Cross Country, he and I talked long and hard about making the gas tank so you could cut a pizza slice out of it and make it a much narrower tank for a different bike."

A sliced and diced Cross Country tank became the fresh tank of the Judge, and it could be made using existing tooling.

"The High-Ball was one of our best-handling bikes because of the tire choice and size combined with the slight chase in fork angle and wheelbase," Brew said. "We put drag bars on one. We put low-rise bars on one. Then we put the CORE bars on it and were like, 'that's close.'"

To complement the CORE bars, the lower controls—with mere pegs, not floorboards—were positioned rearward as mid-mount controls. A new seat was also developed to coordinate with the bars and lower controls and create sporty, performance-minded ergonomics.

The tires—140 in the rear and a 130 up front—provided nicely balanced handling, and their white lettering was a fitting nod to the muscle car era. With the powerful Freedom 106-ci engine, the Judge was nailing the "performance" target. Side covers with oval surfaces that could serve as race bike number plates worked beautifully with the package.

But those side covers met resistance from management in project reviews—reviews where approval was needed to keep the project alive. "They had a hard time with the fact that the bike had a number plate," Brew said, but the development team pushed back. "If you don't have the number plate, you don't have the seat," he said. "And if you don't have the seat, you don't have the bike."

The plate design survived, and the Judge proved very popular in early focus groups, where it struck avid riders as an appealing bike that looked like it would be fun to ride.

It *was* fun to ride—really, really fun—but at bike shows and in dealerships, its ergonomics proved problematic. Customers liked the look of the bike, but when they sat on it, the common—almost unanimous—feedback was that they wanted the bars pulled back at least two inches and the lower controls set forward as well.

Like the SportCruiser (which was also purchased by a small but loyal number of owners), the Judge, introduced in early 2012, never clicked with North American riders. (The Judge was offered in its original form for several more years in Europe.)

The model year 2013 Judge riding position actually promoted a rider's awareness and had the rider more engaged, instead of sitting back as if just along for the ride. But the majority of cruiser customers preferred a bike with "relaxed" and "comfortable" ergonomics—like those of the Vegas.

The Judge was an incredibly fun bike with great power for its size and really nimble handling—it was a blast to ride. But the market rejected the 2012–2013 model with its sporty ergonomics.

Victory offered dealers accessories that included more traditional buckhorn handlebars and a lower control repositioning kit. This book's author took part in an on-road focus group conducted by Victory in Florida in December 2012 to evaluate the Judge's ergonomics. Riders took short rides on three Judge models set up three different ways: the sporty original Judge setup, a slightly more relaxed riding position, and a fully relaxed (2014) position. Two full days of evaluation rides were scheduled and run, but by the time the second group of three riders completed their rides, the consensus was clear: riders absolutely hated the sporty setup and loved the eventual 2014 positioning.

For 2014, the bike was reworked so that its ergonomics were virtually identical to those of a Vegas. The seat and side covers were also reworked, meaning the number plates were gone. What a shame. A great bike that unfortunately didn't connect with enough buyers underwent a soul-crushing reboot to broaden its appeal. It was a shame that the Judge name stayed on the bike for that second year because it was *not* the Judge as it was originally intended to be.

Despite the changes, the Judge's first-year reputation of bad ergonomics lingered. It did not sell well enough in North America to earn a third year on the market. The bike—with its original ergonomics—*did* sell in foreign markets through model year 2017.

The Judge introduced the new designs for the ignition and EFI covers (the previous designs were called "Cheese Wedges" by Victory riders). The 2013 Judge colors were: Gloss Black, Sunset Red, Suede Nuclear Sunset; 2014 Colors: Gloss Black, Gloss Havasu Red. The 2013 Judge (solid black) listed for $13,999.

Model Name	Judge
Production Years	2013–2014
Length	92.1 inches
Wheelbase	64.8 inches
Seat Height	25.9 inches
Ground Clearance	4.7 inches
Dry Weight	660 pounds
Engine	Victory 106-ci Freedom Engine
Exhaust	Staggered slash-cut dual exhaust with crossover
Final Drive	Belt-drive
Fuel Capacity	4.7 U.S. gallons
Front Suspension	Conventional telescopic forks, 43mm diameter; 5.1 inches of travel
Front Brakes	300mm floating rotor with four-piston caliper
Rear Suspension	Single mono-tube gas shock, cast-aluminum swingarm with rising rate linkage, spring preload adjustability, 3.0 inches of travel
Rear Brakes	300mm floating rotor with two-piston caliper
Front Wheel	16.0×3.5-inch cast-aluminum wheel
Rear Wheel	16.0×3.5-inch cast-aluminum wheel
Front Tire	Dunlop 491 E2-RWL 130/90 B16 67H
Rear Tire	Dunlop 491 E2-RWL 140/90 B16 77H
Frame	Tubular steel; uses the engine as a stressed member
Instrumentation	Electronic speedometer with odometer, resettable tripmeter, high-beam indicator, oil light, turn signal indicators, low-fuel light, and low-voltage light
Lights	Twin-beam headlight, turn signals (front and rear), tail/brake light
Paint Colors	See Appendix C: Judge

Boardwalk

Wait, that's a Victory? The Boardwalk was introduced for 2013 at the same time the brand changed its logo from the oval world map to the "V" and bar. With this new logo on a new cruiser that had completely unfamiliar bodywork, the Boardwalk bore almost no resemblance to a Victory.

The Freedom engine was still there, along with the twin right-side exhaust, but that was the extent of recognizable features. Wrapped around its whitewall tires and laced wheels, the Boardwalk had full fenders unlike any previous Victory (the Kingpin fenders had flared out).

The side covers, the ignition and EFI covers, and fuel tank would have been familiar—*if* your crystal ball had showed you what a reworked 2014 Judge would look like. Actually, the Boardwalk *was* the Judge—with wrap-around fenders and beach bar handlebars. They had the same: seat height, wheelbase,

The Boardwalk and the new Victory "V" logo were introduced simultaneously. Combining that logo with the wrap-around fenders, and at first the bike was not particularly recognizable as a Victory. But with a rolling chassis nearly identical to that of the Judge, it was a great bike to ride. *Victory*

rake and trail, ground clearance, overall length, fuel tank, seat (second-generation Judge seat), and front tire. The Judge was too good a bike, too great a rolling chassis for Victory to abandon, so it was essentially repackaged for North America as the Boardwalk.

To give the Boardwalk some distinctive style beyond its unique fenders, it had beach bars that were marketed as "comfortable." But if you check accessories sales, or scan a rally parking lot, you'll see that beach bars aren't all *that* popular.

With its 25.9-inch seat height and smooth ride and handling, the Boardwalk was marketed as an ideal, confidence-inspiring solo bike for a shorter or less-experienced rider. But the beach bars, better suited for tall, long-limbed riders, didn't work for all riders.

Despite this criticism, the Boardwalk was a great bike to ride. Its power-to-weight ratio was impressive, it was comfortable (if your reach gave you command over the beach bars), and it rode and handled beautifully. But its showroom appeal and sales were unimpressive.

After two years on the market, this unfamiliar "Is it really a Victory?" model failed to gain sales traction. This was too bad because it was further proof that Victory engineering could really build terrific cruisers—fun, powerful, smooth-riding bikes. Unfortunately, it seemed the Boardwalk sparked more questions than buyer interest.

The bike debuted in 2013 in two "colors": solid black and Pearl White. For 2014, with most Victory dealers sitting on carryover 2013 inventory, the bike was produced only in two-tone Gloss Black and Sunset Red. A black 2013 Boardwalk had a list price of $15,499 ($15,899 for Pearl White), and the price dropped for 2014 to $14,999.

Victory considered a Boardwalk "reboot" to give the bike more sales appeal. One idea was to have leading custom builders produce special versions of the bike. Scott Kietzmann of Conquest Customs embraced this vision and came up with the powerful custom idea seen in this concept drawing. However, no such bikes were ever built for Victory.

Courtesy of Conquest Customs

For 2014, the Boardwalk's second and final year in production, the bike was available in this two-tone paint scheme. Despite a richer look than the original solid black and solid white options, the Boardwalk wasn't popular enough to earn a third year. *Victory*

Model Name	Boardwalk	**Rear Brakes**	300mm floating rotor with two-piston caliper
Production Years	2013–2014		
Length	96.7 inches	**Front Wheel**	16.0×3.5-inch cast-aluminum wheel
Wheelbase	64.8 inches	**Rear Wheel**	16.0×3.5-inch cast-aluminum wheel
Seat Height	25.9 inches	**Front Tire**	Metzeler ME880, 130/90-16 67H
Ground Clearance	4.7 inches	**Rear Tire**	Metzeler ME880, 150/80B-16 71H
Dry Weight	675 pounds	**Frame**	Tubular steel; uses the engine as a stressed member
Engine	Victory 106-ci Freedom Engine		
Exhaust	Staggered slash-cut dual exhaust with crossover	**Instrumentation**	Electronic speedometer with odometer, resettable tripmeter, high-beam indicator, oil light, turn signal indicators, low-fuel light, and low-voltage light
Final Drive	Belt-drive		
Fuel Capacity	4.7 U.S. gallons		
Front Suspension	Conventional telescopic forks, 43mm diameter; 5.1 inches of travel		
Front Brakes	300mm floating rotor with four-piston caliper	**Lights**	Twin-beam headlight, turn signals (front and rear), tail/brake light
Rear Suspension	Single mono-tube gas shock, cast-aluminum swingarm with rising rate linkage, spring preload adjustability, 3.0 inches of travel	**Paint Colors**	Gloss Black, Pearl White (2013)

Gunner

If you liked the High-Ball—this book's authors were among its biggest fans—you would love the Gunner. The Gunner was essentially the High-Ball with low, traditional handlebars and different wheels. Beyond that, the Gunner was, like the High-Ball, a no-frills, powerful, smooth-riding cruiser. Had Victory stayed in business, this single platform could have served as the brand's lone cruiser platform, with a customer's choice of apes or standard handlebars. It was that good of a bike. Like the Vegas, there would never be any reason to leave it out of the model line.

In March 2014, Jamie Elvidge reviewed the bike for *Cycle World* and called it "basically a Judge wearing new 24-spoke cast-aluminum shoes, and a tiny skirt instead of a robe, but for a parts-bin bike, it looks very much like its own animal. A dark, muscular one that turns heads and prompts questions."

We contend that the bike shared its rolling chassis with the High-Ball, not the Judge, but we agree with her assessment of the Gunner's performance and handling. She wrote:

"This is a chassis and drivetrain I know very well, so as expected, I loved running the Gunner around Daytona, and especially down some of the backroads that allow for extended romping. The Freedom 106 is a very lovable motor, with heaps of hair-tingling torque (we measured 96 pound-feet when we had the 2013 Judge on the Cycle World *Dynojet dyno, with a respectable 81 horses to further harvest momentum). It's a real head-snapper, the 106, and the sweet snarl emitted by the blacked-out, stock dual exhaust encourages you to abuse the throttle just for grins.*

"The chassis is solid in feel, and though it features a low look and a low 25-inch seat height, the Gunner won't grind pegs near as easily as some of Victory's more chopper-esque models. Steering feel is not at all heavy, and tracking through corners is optimum

The Gunner was essentially a High-Ball with traditional-height handlebars, meaning it was a fantastic ride and a winner from the day it hit the market. The bike was available in Suede Titanium Metallic in its first year (2015). *Victory*

The 2015 Gunner's dry weight was 649 pounds—220 pounds lighter than that year's Vision—yet the proven Freedom 106/6 powered both bikes, meaning Gunner riders enjoyed an incredible power-to-weight experience. *Victory*

for such a big cruiser. The transmission is also what we already know: industrial in feel, very loud, but with true shifts and no hunting for neutral. Braking scores for this big bobber are only decent, and would be much improved by an additional 300mm disc to match the single unit currently used up front. A single 300mm disc is also used to control the rear wheel."

The Gunner shared classic styling with the Vegas as both had the split-tail fuel tank, the same side covers and rear fender, and the traditional "cheese wedge" ignition and EFI covers.

The Gunner was in the model lineup from 2014-2017. The first year, it was available only in Suede Titanic Metallic with graphics, and for the final three years, it was also available in Suede Green Metallic with graphics. The green version resembled the Olive Drab used on military vehicles, so it was typically the chosen bike to feature in Victory projects supporting IAVA, Iraq and Afghanistan Veterans of America.

Along with power and a great ride, it delivered solid value: The 2014 Gunner U.S. MSRP was $12,999. As Elvidge wrote: "For many, the jury is

The Gunner was a no-frills cruiser that delivered style, comfort, value, and outstanding performance. *Victory*

still out on whether this lightly restyled Judge is a truly a bobber or just another way for Victory to spin its barrel full of Big Twins. But at $12,999 (that's a grand less than the Judge and five hundred below the High-Ball) it's surely one big wannabe bobber of a bargain."

The paint of the Suede Green Metallic Gunner was similar to the green paint traditionally used on Army vehicles, which made the green Gunner *the* choice for Victory's promotions with Iraq and Afghanistan Veterans of America (IAVA). These veterans rode a fleet of Victory motorcycles, including this Gunner, in the 2015 Veterans Day parade in New York City. *Victory*

Model Name	Gunner	**Rear Brakes**	300mm floating rotor with two-piston caliper
Production Years	2014–2017		
Length	92.5 inches	**Front Wheel**	16.0×3.5-inch cast-aluminum wheel
Wheelbase	64.8 inches	**Rear Wheel**	16.0×3.5-inch cast-aluminum wheel
Seat Height	25.0 inches	**Front Tire**	Dunlop 491 E2-RWL 130/90 B16 67H
Ground Clearance	4.7 inches	**Rear Tire**	Dunlop 491 E2-RWL 140/90 B16 77H
Dry Weight	660 pounds	**Frame**	Tubular steel; uses the engine as a stressed member
Engine	Victory 106-ci Freedom Engine		
Exhaust	Staggered slash-cut dual exhaust with crossover	**Instrumentation**	Electronic speedometer with odometer, resettable tripmeter, high-beam indicator, oil light, turn signal indicators, low-fuel light, and low-voltage light
Final Drive	Belt-drive		
Fuel Capacity	4.5 U.S. gallons		
Front Suspension	Conventional telescopic forks, 43mm diameter; 5.1 inches of travel		
Front Brakes	300mm floating rotor with four-piston caliper	**Lights**	Twin-beam headlight, turn signals (front and rear), tail/brake light
Rear Suspension	Single mono-tube gas shock, cast-aluminum swingarm with rising rate linkage, spring preload adjustability, 3.0 inches of travel	**Paint Colors**	Suede Titanium Metallic with graphics (2014)

Empulse TT

There should be a big asterisk next to this bike's name in a book about Victory. There's not really much Victory DNA in this sporty, all-electric model, but it joined the Victory family through a business acquisition.

In 2011, Polaris bought into Brammo, the electric vehicle and electric energy source company based in Oregon. In 2015, Polaris fully acquired Brammo's electric motorcycle business, so the Brammo electric motorcycle became a Polaris bike, and was branded as a Victory, not an Indian.

The investments made sense for Polaris, which had one division producing electric utility vehicles (Global Electric Motorcars, or GEM), and was no doubt exploring alternative power solutions for future off-road vehicles, utility vehicles, and motorcycles.

Brammo had been producing its Empulse R motorcycle for about five years when Polaris acquired the Brammo bike business. Victory engineers worked with the Brammo team to enhance the bike as much as possible without re-engineering it from scratch, and the Empulse TT was in the Victory lineup for 2016 and 2017 (virtually unchanged from year to year).

The Empulse TT was a sporty, impressively powerful bike with overall performance akin to that of a 600 sport bike. It featured sport bike ergonomics and suspension, premium Brembo brakes (dual discs up front), chain-drive, a six-speed transmission (with two gears down and four up), and an electric motor. The motor was rated for 54 hp and 61 foot-pound of torque.

The bike was nimble, had outstanding braking, and had absolutely linear throttle response: the more

After Polaris acquired Brammo's electric motorcycle business in 2015, Victory and Brammo engineers worked on the Brammo Empulse R and brought it to market as the Victory Empulse TT. Along with its outstanding power, the bike had absolutely linear acceleration and power delivery. *Victory*

The Empulse TT had some premium components, including Brembo brakes with dual front discs and adjustable rear suspension. What it didn't have was extended riding range on a full battery charge. Depending on how aggressively it was ridden, the bike could get about 65 to 100 miles from a full charge. *Victory*

you twisted it, the faster you went. But, the more you twisted it, the faster you consumed the battery power, which was one of the bike's two drawbacks. The bike could be run in SPORT or ECO mode, with the latter reducing the available-energy ceiling to optimize the range of the battery charge.

With the battery packs fully charged, the bike had a range of about 60 to 100 miles. Ride it however you like in SPORT mode, with no concern for conserving energy, and you might cover about 60 miles. Put it in ECO and ride conservatively and you might approach 100 miles. From zero charge, it took eight hours to fully recharge the batteries; an accessory charger that used 220-volt power was available, and it cut charging time in half.

Limited range was a drawback to the Empulse TT, as was the MSRP: $19,999. These were such

significant drawbacks that Victory retail sales never reached double digits in two years. (The bikes were not carried by every dealer. Victory wanted the bikes available in densely populated metro areas with upscale customers who embraced advanced technology.) Once the Victory wind down was announced, some dealers were selling Empulse TTs for under $9,000.

Look for an electric motorcycle from Indian in the near future. And look for Polaris to possibly utilize Brammo power and technology in a wide range of vehicles in the future.

The Empulse TT is the only Victory model not produced exclusively at the Spirit Lake, Iowa, final assembly plant. A couple units were assembled there as a test run, but the majority were produced at Brammo's Oregon facility.

Race-prepped versions of the Empulse carried riders to podium finishes at the 2015 and 2016 Isle of Man TT. The bike's power delivery was tuned so a racer could run at full throttle as much as possible and have just enough battery power to complete the one-lap race around the island. *Victory*

Model Name	Empulse TT	**Rear Wheel**	16.0×4.5-inch cast-aluminum wheel
Production Years	2016–2017	**Front Tire**	Continental Sport Attack II 120/70 ZR17 58W
Length	81.2 inches		
Wheelbase	58.0 inches	**Rear Tire**	Continental Sport Attack II 160/60 ZR17 69W
Seat Height	31.4 inches		
Ground Clearance	7.29 inches	**Frame**	Tubular steel
Dry Weight	470 pounds	**Instrumentation**	LCD display, speedometer, tachometer, gear position, energy consumption, battery status, estimated range, and system status
Engine	Electric motor		
Exhaust	NA		
Final Drive	Chain-drive		
Fuel Capacity	NA	**Lights**	Twin-beam headlight, turn signals (front and rear), tail/brake light
Front Suspension	Adjustable 43mm inverted forks		
Front Brakes	Dual 310mm Brembo floating rotors with twin four-piston calipers	**Paint Colors**	Titanium Silver with Havasu Red (2016)
Rear Suspension	Adjustable direct-acting shock		
Rear Brakes	Single rotor with two-piston caliper		
Front Wheel	17.0×3.5-inch cast-aluminum wheel		

Octane

Despite statements from Polaris officials that Victory and Indian would not share components, the Octane was a joint venture with a shared foundation—and it made sense. The Octane and the Indian Scout (as well as the Scout Sixty and Bobber) each turned out distinct enough to be stand-alone models.

The bikes shared a similar frame and had the transmission and driveline in common. Victory product manager Brandon Kraemer told *Cycle World* that the Scout and Octane "only share about thirty-five percent of their parts, however, either on a part-number or a part-cost basis. We wanted to leverage the parts that weren't super customer-facing, like the axle shafts. But anything that gives the bike its character is unique."

Each brand's design and engineering team: finished off the engine with cylinders and top ends of

The Octane had the first truly liquid-cooled engine in Victory history. All early engines and Freedom engines had been air-cooled, with oil circulated to assist in heat transfer. Radiator styling is always iffy, but Victory managed to house the Octane radiator with style. *Victory*

The Victory Stunt Team impressed audiences with their Octane stunts, which included taillight-shattering wheelies, drifting, and tire-destroying burnouts. *Author*

their choice, established their own ergonomics, and added brand-specific styling.

The Indian Scout was in the brand's 2015 model lineup, while the Victory Octane was held and, frankly, overhyped before it was unveiled in February 2016. Victory's pre-introductory tease campaign led riders to believe they might be climbing on a bike like the Project 156 rocket that was raced up Pikes Peak.

Instead, Victory presented the Octane, which some observers understandably called the "Victory Scout." As Lance Oliver wrote for RevZilla.com in February 2016: "[A]s for the Octane itself, I'll be damned if it doesn't look a lot like a lightly buffed Indian Scout in Victory clothing. Or, to be more accurate, an Indian Scout with the cylinders bored out five millimeters, four additional horsepower, and different size wheels."

But the Octane benefited from being second to market. Early Scout production models had some internal mechanical gremlins, such as balky fuel delivery, and all such issues were sorted out before the Octane hit the market, ready to roast some rear tires.

Victory's demo ride fleet at Daytona Bike Week 2016 included about 20 Octanes that were tested continuously by riders, eager to see if the bike could match its hype. Most riders were highly impressed, and virtually all who rode the Scout and Octane back-to-back named the Octane as the faster bike. Plus, they saw the Victory stunt team, which performed next to the demo site, shred tires and perform wheelies, stoppies, and more on their Octanes.

The Octane had a 1179cc (46cc more than the Scout) liquid-cooled V-twin that produced 104 hp and 76 foot-pound of torque (compared to 100 hp and 72 foot-pound for the Scout). Ready for riding, the Octane weighed 548 pounds, and unlike other Victory models, the Octane's final belt drive was on the left side of the bike.

Like so many Victory cruisers, the Octane had its exhaust pipes stacked on the right side of the bike. Unlike all other Victory models, though, the bike had its final-drive belt on the left side. *Victory*

The Octane had a 25.9-inch seat height, the handlebars were nearly straight drag bars, and the lower controls were in a slightly forward position. Steve Anderson of *Cycle World* offered more details:

"Wrapped around the engine is a chassis that stretches out to a 61.6-inch wheelbase. The front tire is a beefy 130/70-18, while the rear is a relatively sporty 160/70-17. A single disc brake is used at the front. The steering head rakes out at 29 degrees and works with 5.1 inches of trail, standard figures for a cruiser where good handling is more important than an extreme raked-out appearance. The fork allows 5.1 inches of wheel travel, while the twin rear shocks permit only 3.0 inches of rear-wheel movement—again, not an unusual number for a cruiser where seat height concerns and 'low' style can trump rider comfort on a bad road."

The Octane was designed and marketed for sporty riding, not stretched-out long-distance cruising. Anderson noted it could quickly hit triple digits:

"As with the Indian Scout, the Octane's engine makes the first impression: sweet! . . . The bike charges through first gear, reaching the rev limiter at about 45 mph, and pulls hard through second and third. One hundred miles per hour comes quickly. But even more impressive is how smoothly the bike pulls in the midrange and from low speeds; leaving it in sixth,

you could lug it down to 1,250 rpm, open the throttle, and (assisted by ECU-controlled throttle-by-wire) pull smoothly back up to highway speed. Similarly, this might be a 1,179cc twin with big pistons, but only the ghost of engine vibration ever reaches the rider. At 65 mph on the freeway, it's almost glassy smooth. At 75 to 80 mph, that ghost of a buzz touches you lightly, mostly through the pegs and slightly through the grips, but only enough to let you know you're being propelled by an engine and not enough to annoy."

The original Octane, listed as a 2017 model, was available only in Matte Super Steel Gray and had a U.S. MSRP of $10,499. At mid-year in 2016, the 2017 models were introduced in the original color as well as Suede Pearl White, Gloss Black with Graphics, and Gloss Black. The Gloss Black bike had a U.S. MSRP of $9,999.

Three Pre-Production Specials

The extended run-up to the Octane's introduction included three "raw, adrenaline-fueled concepts [that] influenced Octane," according to Victory. They were the Project 156 bike, built by Roland Sands Design to race in the Pikes Peak Hill Climb; "Ignition," a custom built by Swiss racer and custom builder Urs Erbacher; and "Combustion," the Zach Ness-designed custom that was a powerful, stripped version of the Octane.

Model Name	Octane
Production Years	2016–2017
Length	90.9 inches
Wheelbase	62.1 inches
Seat Height	25.9 inches
Ground Clearance	5.3 inches
Dry Weight	528 pounds
Engine	Victory 1200cc Octane Engine
Exhaust	Dual slash-cut mufflers with common volume
Final Drive	Belt-drive
Fuel Capacity	3.4 U.S. gallons
Front Suspension	41mm damper-tube forks with dual-rate springs, 4.7 inches of travel
Front Brakes	298mm disc with dual-piston caliper
Rear Suspension	Twin shocks with dual-rate springs, adjustable preload, 3.0 inches of travel
Rear Brakes	298mm disc with single-piston caliper
Front Wheel	18×3.5 inch 10-spoke cast-aluminum wheel
Rear Wheel	17×4.5 inch 10-spoke cast-aluminum wheel
Front Tire	130/70-18 63H Kenda tire
Rear Tire	160/70-17 76H Kenda tire
Frame	Cast-aluminum and twin-tube steel construction
Instrumentation	Electronic speedometer with tachometer, odometer, resettable tripmeter, high-beam indicator, oil light, turn signal indicators, low-fuel light, and low-voltage light
Lights	Twin-beam headlight, turn signals (front and rear), tail/brake light
Paint Colors	Matte Super Steel Gray (2016)

CHAPTER 6

The Baggers

In the Victory definition of bike categories, a bagger had saddlebags, no trunk, and the front end could include a fairing, windshield, or no wind protection. The V92C Deluxe could be considered the first Victory bagger, but the V92TC was the most legit early bagger. The Kingpin Deluxe was a bagger (covered in chapter 5), as were Vision models such as the Vision Street and Vision 8-Ball (covered in chapter 7).

But the golden age of Victory baggers arrived in model year 2010 with the introduction of the Cross Country and Cross Roads. These bikes were so outstanding, especially the extremely versatile Cross Country, that it's possible the brand's history could have been altered significantly if the Cross Country had reached market before the Vision.

From 2012 through 2017, Cross bikes were Victory's best-seller models—including the strong-selling Cross Country Tour. While specific model numbers were not available, the Cross bike production breakdown was about 55% Cross Country–style baggers and 45% Cross Country Tours. Fueling the Tour's appeal was its versatility (the trunk could be removed easily), and the fact that buying the fully equipped Tour was a better value than buying a Cross Country and purchasing the trunk as an accessory for around $1,750 or $1,800.

Cross Country

Known as "the Cross bikes," the Cross Country, Cross Roads, and related variations represented Victory's maturation as a premium motorcycle manufacturer. Their shared rolling chassis was a work of two-wheeled art, offering a comfortable ride, smooth handling, a strong and durable platform for two-up riding and cargo hauling, and tremendous versatility.

The Cross Country achieved the greatest and most-enduring success of all Victory baggers, undergoing only minimal change since it was introduced for model year 2010, and never dropping out of the model lineup the way other Cross-platform baggers did.

This was because the Cross Country offered the combination of features the largest market segment of riders wanted most: great performance, ample cargo space, two-up capabilities, and a fairing with an audio system.

Victory learned a great deal in developing the Vision's two-piece cast-aluminum frame, and the Cross bikes used a slightly downsized version of that

Victory nailed it in 2015 with its lowered and customized Cross Country, the Magnum (a 2016 model is seen here). Riders loved the low-slung style and ride, especially when they added a set of mini ape handlebars. *Brian J. Nelson*

design. (The front of the Cross bikes' frame did not serve as the engine's air intake as it did on the Vision.) The Cross-bike frame was lightweight yet strong, and gave Victory design and engineer teams abundant options as they finished off the new generation of baggers.

In the case of the Cross Country, the most appealing features were: the proven Freedom 106/6 V-Twin, comfortable two-up seat, cruise control, ABS braking (on most but not all Cross Country models over the years), spacious and lockable hard saddlebags, and a fork-mounted fairing that hosted the bike's instrumentation, audio system, and fixed-position windshield. Importantly, the saddlebags were more traditionally styled—boxy and clearly added onto the bike—than the smooth, integrated side storage compartments of the Vision. These Cross Country bags, along with the Cross Country fuel tank, gave the bike a far more traditional—and marketable—look than the Vision.

Among the Cross Country's impressive numbers were:

- 21 gallons of cargo space in the lockable, weather-sealed hard saddlebags
- 580-pound load capacity
- 14-inch-long driver floorboards (plus floorboards for the passenger)
- 5.8-gallon fuel capacity for excellent range
- 4.7 inches of rear suspension travel from the rear suspension comprised of an adjustable air shock and coil spring

John Burns of *Cycle World* rode the Cross Country at a press introduction in Texas and reported:

"With no downtubes, the aluminum frame lets the Cross bikes carry Victory's usual 106-cubic-inch 50-degree V-Twin nice and low, and the seats on the new bikes are likewise a mere 26.2 inches from the

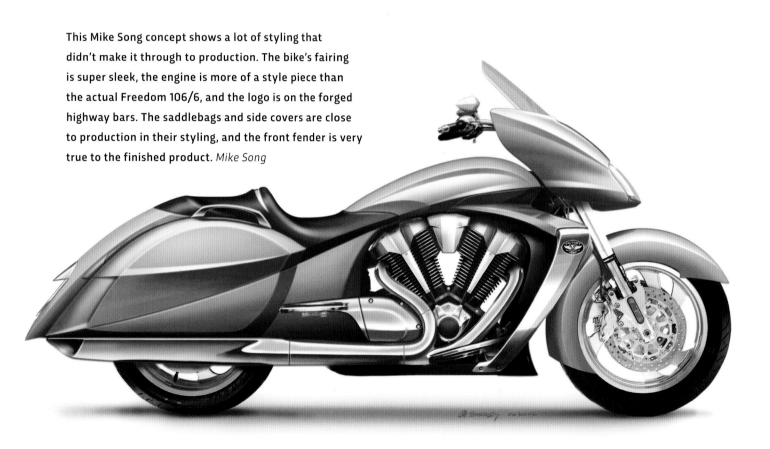

This Mike Song concept shows a lot of styling that didn't make it through to production. The bike's fairing is super sleek, the engine is more of a style piece than the actual Freedom 106/6, and the logo is on the forged highway bars. The saddlebags and side covers are close to production in their styling, and the front fender is very true to the finished product. *Mike Song*

Senior Staff Industrial Designer Mike Song compares the clay model of the Cross Country to the concept artwork on the wall behind the model. Full-size models such as this use real components, including the engine, forks, and front wheel and tire to give the model accurate proportions. *Mike Song*

pavement. Even at that low elevation, there's a nicely plush yet well-controlled 4.7 inches of rear-suspension travel, with air-adjustable preload similar to that used on the Vision. For 'touring' baggers, the Cross bikes can actually be hustled along at a reasonably rapid pace, with that aluminum frame/stressed-engine chassis keeping the wheels in good alignment and aimed in the intended direction quite nicely over some of Texas' finest twisty pavement; you're going at a pretty good clip when the floorboards let you know to chill a little. And when you're just cruising, 3,000 rpm on the tach nets a nice, relaxed-feeling 80 mph."

Brian Harley, writing for Motorcycle-usa.com, wrote:

"The Victory Cross Country, like the Vision, handles surprisingly easy for a big touring bike. Its fork-mounted fairing is lightweight plastic so it doesn't affect steering and the feel at the bars is light. It's not a load to navigate at parking lot speeds thanks to a low 26.5-inch seat height and a wheelbase that is 1.8

inches tighter (67.5 to 65.7 inch) than the [Yamaha] Stratoliner S. The chassis is very stable while exploring the bagger's lean angles. An inverted 43mm fork keeps the front end planted. Once it's leaned over, it doesn't waver until you're ready to stand it up and accelerate out of a turn. The Cross Country's back end is stabilized by an air shock and coil spring that can be adjusted for loads using a small hand-held air shock pump which connects to the bike's right side."

Along with its distinctive fairing styling, the Cross Country originally distinguished itself visually with forged highway bars. They were initially plated for a bright finish, and in later years came with color-matched paint. The broad, forged bars received mixed reviews initially, but when the Cross Country received traditional round-tube highway bars in 2013, some riders missed the model's unique original tip-overs.

Over the years, Cross Country models were painted and equipped to slot into several popular bagger price points, meaning that most, but not every unit, had cruise control or ABS braking. The best

This photo includes style lines and comments made by the industrial design team for the stylists shaping the clay model.

Mike Song

This naked Cross Roads shows the rear of the frame, which hosts the seats and, at the rear, a supplemental support plate for the exhaust pipes that have rubber pads used as perches for the saddlebags. The air line extending through the hole atop the frame is for the air shock.

Author

ones had cruise control because the bike was a dream on the open road, and that feature made all-day rides extra enjoyable.

As with the Vision, the Cross Country's handlebar-mounted controls for the audio system and cruise control were boxy, bolt-on units. However, Victory was developing a cleaner set of control cubes with integrated audio and cruise controls, but was interrupted by the announcement of the brand's end. Adapted versions of these cubes were introduced on 2018 Indian Motorcycle models.

The most popular accessories for Cross Country models included a Stage 1 exhaust with a throatier exhaust note, windshields of various heights and styles, fork-mounted lower air deflectors, saddlebag liners, and a Lock & Ride (no tools required) passenger backrest. As early as 2011, the model's second year on the market, the Lock & Ride trunk was available as an accessory; it was standard equipment on the Cross Country Tour introduced in 2012.

When introduced in 2010, Cross Country U.S. MSRPs were: $17,999 (solid black), $18,599 (Midnight Cherry), and $19,499 (Black & Graphite with Extreme Skulls). The 2011 MSRP was $17,999, the list price in

Victory offered premium paint schemes for the 2014 Cross Country models, which were produced in low numbers and were therefore like unlabeled limited-edition models. *Victory*

2013 and 2014 was $18,999, and the base (solid black) 2017 model's MSRP was $19,499.

Factory Custom Paint

In 2014, Victory offered limited numbers of Factory Custom Paint models with gorgeous paint schemes. For $20,499, the Cross Country was available with these Factory Custom Paint options: Two-Tone Boss Blue & Gloss Black, Two-Tone Suede Supersteel & Black, Suede Silver With Flames, and Tequila Gold With Flames. Victory used this paint program as a soft intro to its next-level custom bagger: The Magnum, which was introduced in 2015.

Model Name	Cross Country
Production Years	2010–2017
Length	104.4 inches
Wheelbase	65.7 inches
Seat Height	26.25 inches
Ground Clearance	5.8 inches
Dry Weight	765 pounds
Engine	Victory 106-ci Freedom Engine
Exhaust	Split dual exhaust with crossover
Final Drive	Belt-drive
Fuel Capacity	5.8 U.S. gallons
Front Suspension	Inverted cartridge telescopic forks, 43mm diameter; 5.1 inches of travel
Front Brakes	Dual 300mm floating rotors with four-piston caliper; ABS
Rear Suspension	Single mono-tube gas shock, cast-aluminum swingarm with constant rate linkage; adjustable air spring; 4.7 inches of travel
Rear Brakes	300mm floating rotor with two-piston caliper
Front Wheel	18.0×3.0-inch cast-aluminum wheel
Rear Wheel	16.0×5.0-inch cast-aluminum wheel
Front Tire	130/70R18 Dunlop Elite 3
Rear Tire	180/60R16 Dunlop Elite 3
Frame	Cast-aluminum frame; uses the engine as a stressed member
Instrumentation	Analog speedometer and LCD that displays: tachometer, clock (time of day), gear position, diagnostic readouts, and warning lights; plus stand-alone fuel gauge
Lights	Twin-beam headlight, turn signals (front and rear), tail/brake light
Paint Colors	See Appendix C: Cross Country

Ness Signature Series Cross Country

The Cross Country was the base model of the Cory Ness Signature Series Cross Country in 2011 and 2012, as well as the 2013 Zach Ness Signature Series model. Each featured a custom paint scheme, Ness Graphics, and numerous accessories as standard equipment. The penultimate Ness model ever offered was a 2014 Cross Country, which was styled by the three Nesses and had Ness logos on the saddlebags.

Model Name   Ness Signature Series Cross Country
Production Years   2011–2014
Paint Colors   See Appendix C: Ness Signature Series Models

Note: *Except for special features, such as custom wheels and cosmetic accessories (covers, controls, etc.), refer to the Cross Country specifications for model details.*

The final Ness Signature Series model was a Cross Country styled collaboratively by Arlen, Cory, and Zach Ness for model year 2014. The Ness logo appears on the side covers. *Victory*

Cross Country 8-Ball

In model years 2014–2016, Victory offered the Cross Country 8-Ball for $17,999, about $1,000 less than a gloss black standard model. The 8-Ball was an impressive value because not much had been removed from the standard bike. It had the same engine, seating, saddlebags, and fairing, but there were no highway bars, and there was no audio source. The speakers were still in the fairing, but an MP3 device or other source was required.

Model Name   Cross Country 8-Ball
Production Years   2014–2016
Paint Colors   Black
Note: *Refer to standard Cross Country specifications for model details.*

The Cross Country 8-Ball was an impressive value. Very little was deleted on this blacked-out model, except an audio source and cruise control. (It also lacked ABS, but so did selected "standard" Cross Country models.) *Victory*

Victory Police Motorcycles

The Cross Country served as the foundation of the Commander I and the Stealth Commander I Victory Police Motorcycle (VPM) models. VPM was an Arizona-based company—independently owned and operated; not a Polaris subsidiary—whose front man in the field was Mike Schultz, a former Victory dealer in the state. VPM purchased bikes from Victory and equipped them with whatever electronics and special equipment law enforcement agencies wanted. The equipment could include lights, sirens, skid plates, firearms holders, storage boxes, adjustable windshields, branded case covers, and more. Schultz and VPM had several dozen client agencies across North America riding Victory motorcycles, including the high-profile Daytona Beach P.D. (VPM models were also built using the Vision, Cross Roads, and in the company's earliest days, the Kingpin as the base models. The overwhelming majority of the police bikes, however, were Cross Country build-outs.)

Model Name	Victory Police Motorcycles [Cross Country]
Production Years	2010–2017
Paint Colors	Custom painted to individual law enforcement agencies' specifications

Here's a Cross Country converted into a police motorcycle for the Lethbridge Police Service in Alberta, Canada. The police bikes were typically equipped with lights and a siren, a rear-mounted storage/electrical box, tipover protection, and, if desired, weapons scabbards, adjustable windshields, and skid plates. *VPM*

Cross Roads

Bagger riders wanted music, and they wanted some of the conveniences included in fairings, meaning they wanted the Cross Country—not the Cross Roads. Introduced with the Cross Country for 2010, the Cross Roads had the same rolling chassis but no fairing. This meant the Cross Roads did not have audio, and its instrumentation was a single multi-function gauge like that of Victory cruisers at the time.

The Cross Roads could be equipped with an accessory windshield and there were even aftermarket audio systems available, but that wasn't appealing enough for many riders. For this reason, the Cross Roads lagged far behind its faired sibling in sales.

The 2010 Cross Roads came with the same hard saddlebags as the Cross Country and had a U.S. MSRP of $15,999 (solid black). In 2011 and 2012, a Cross Roads buyer determined the bike's makeup (see below); the 2011 list price was $14,999 for a black bike, and it was $15,999 for 2012, the final year for the standard Cross Roads. A Cross Roads 8-Ball was available in 2014 for $15,999 with the hard bags, after which the model name was shelved.

For 2011, Victory introduced the CORE Custom program for the Cross Roads. It was an attempt to spark sales of this model by highlighting its versatility and the fact that it could be equipped to suit any type of rider. At the dealership, the customer chose

Introduced for model year 2010, the Cross Roads provided riders with the outstanding ride and handling of the new Cross-bike platform, along with the large, lockable saddlebags. The Cross Roads gave riders an option of a bagger without a fairing; the windshield could be removed easily. *Victory*

The Cross Roads was a great-handling bike. Like all models built on a Victory two-piece cast aluminum frame, the bike handled so well it felt lighter than it was. *Victory*

For 2011, Victory offered forty-eight equipment combinations for the Cross Roads. A rider could select color, saddlebag style, highway bar style (or go without), and whether to ride with or without a windshield. This 2011 Cross Roads has the unique combo of old-school faux leather saddlebags with the highly styled forged highway bars. *Victory*

Cross Roads models were excellent baggers, but the Cross Country models outsold them by such a wide margin that Cross Roads production ended with model year 2012. *Victory*

the Cross Roads' color, type of saddlebags (hard or leather-look), windshield (with or without), and whether to add front and/or rear tip-over protection. The hard bags had a combined cargo capacity of 21 gallons, while the plastic-interior, faux leather-covered bags had 17.4 gallons of space.

With this program, the onus was on Victory dealers to stock the various optional equipment, or to be sharp in re-ordering it to maintain inventory. Unfortunately, the program did not elevate Cross Roads sales significantly because the preference for the Cross Country's fairing with audio and hard bags was so strong.

Model Name	Cross Roads
Production Years	2010–2012
Length	104.4 inches
Wheelbase	65.7 inches
Seat Height	26.25 inches
Ground Clearance	5.8 inches
Dry Weight	745 pounds
Engine	Victory 106-ci Freedom Engine
Exhaust	Split dual exhaust with crossover
Final Drive	Belt-drive
Fuel Capacity	5.8 U.S. gallons
Front Suspension	Inverted cartridge telescopic forks, 43mm diameter; 5.1 inches of travel
Front Brakes	Dual 300mm floating rotors with four-piston caliper; ABS
Rear Suspension	Single mono-tube gas shock, cast-aluminum swingarm with constant rate linkage; adjustable air spring; 4.7 inches of travel
Rear Brakes	300mm floating rotor with two-piston caliper
Front Wheel	18.0×3.0-inch cast-aluminum wheel
Rear Wheel	16.0×5.0-inch cast-aluminum wheel
Front Tire	130/70R18 Dunlop Elite 3
Rear Tire	180/60R16 Dunlop Elite 3
Frame	Cast-aluminum frame; uses the engine as a stressed member
Instrumentation	Electronic speedometer with odometer, resettable tripmeter, high-beam indicator, oil light, turn signal indicators, low-fuel light, and low-voltage light
Lights	Twin-beam headlight, turn signals (front and rear), tail/brake light
Paint Colors	Black, Midnight Cherry (2010)

Cross Roads 8-Ball

The 2014 Cross Roads 8-Ball was probably the ultimate value buy among Victory baggers. As an 8-Ball, it was an all-black bike, and since the standard Cross Roads didn't have many luxury features, there wasn't much to delete to make it an 8-Ball. Although the Cross Roads 8-Ball did not have cruise control nor anti-lock braking, it had virtually everything else, including the great Cross-bike rolling chassis—complete with dual front brake rotors—the lockable hard saddlebags, two-up seating, and adjustable rear air shock. It was an ideal starting point for a customizer or a rider who wanted to get into a premium bagger at the lowest retail price. The 2014 model had a U.S. MSRP of $15,999. That was $3,000 less than a 2014 Cross Country, but apparently not appealing enough to spark sales, which made the Cross Roads 8-Ball a one-and-done model.

Model Name	Cross Roads 8-Ball
Production Years	2014
Paint Colors	Black

Note: *With the exception of cruise control and anti-lock braking (both deleted on this model), specifications are identical to those of the standard Cross Roads.*

The Cross Roads 8-Ball was in the lineup for just one year, 2014. Victory found that bagger buyers didn't want the "naked" Cross Roads, whether it came in colors or in this solid-value, basic black 8-Ball treatment. *Victory*

What the High-Ball's ape hangers did for Victory cruisers, the apes on the 2012 Hard-Ball did for Victory baggers: infused the model segment with a dose of badass attitude. Yet the Hard-Ball was not simply a cosmetic bike. It was an outstanding ride, combining great Cross-bike performance with the comfortable reach to the controls and easy steering leverage of the high bars. *Victory*

Hard-Ball

There might be no stronger evidence of riders' love of audio than the 2013 Hard-Ball. This was a tremendous bike—the outstanding Cross platform, great style with its Matte Black paint and subtle pinstripes, two-up seating, hard saddlebags, and bad-ass ape hangers—but it didn't have the Cross Country's fairing, and thus sales were hard-won. Victory introduced an accessory fairing and accessory fairing audio system, but those add-ons did not integrate with the Hard-Ball's style, and weren't a deal maker.

However, its one year's worth of production was enough to create an avid cult following of Hard-Ball riders, and they're the winners. For several years afterward, riders would ask at demo events and shows if the Hard-Ball were available because its looks blew them away. Sadly, it was a one-and-done model. Its list price in 2013 was $18,999.

The laced wheels coordinated nicely with the bike's style and complemented the old-school ape hangers. With those bars and wheels, the Hard-Ball was the bagger version of the High-Ball. That sounds great, but if riders wanted a Victory bagger, they wanted the Cross Country with its front-end weather protection and its audio system.

The Hard-Ball had everything *except* the fairing and audio, but it didn't attract enough buyers to remain in the lineup. Here's to those lucky bastards who bought one! They're riding a great bike.

Model Name   Hard-Ball
Production Years   2013
Paint Colors   Matte Black with Red Pinstripes
Note: *Refer to Cross Roads specifications for model details. Cruise control and anti-lock braking were standard on the Hard-Ball.*

Only in production for one year, not many words were written about the Hard-Ball. We offer these: Badass. Awesome. *Victory*

In an effort to boost Cross Roads sales, Victory offered the 2013 Cross Roads Classic that had a retro hot rod paint with pinstripe accents, custom-stitched studded seats, "soft saddlebags" (faux leather over plastic interiors), windshield, driving lights, chrome tipovers, fender guards, and 18-inch laced wheels. *Victory*

Cross Roads Classic & Classic LE

Like the Hard-Ball, these adaptations of the Cross Roads look great and ride beautifully—but didn't sell well enough to remain in production. The Classic and Classic LE featured gorgeous two-tone paint with pinstriping as well as faux leather-covered saddlebags for a traditional bagger look.

Despite these features, no fairing meant no audio, which meant not enough Classic buyers. Except for the fairing and audio, these bikes had everything the Cross Country had: comfort, great ride, good power, and smooth handling.

Well, one other thing was missing: lockable saddlebags. The hard bags on Cross Country models had weather-sealed lids that were lockable. That added considerable peace of mind while touring, especially when the bike was parked overnight with tools, rain gear, and more in a bag. The leather-look saddlebags most commonly used on Cross Roads models did not lock, and they offered slightly less cargo space than the hard bags. When a shopper was checking off all the details, these bag deficiencies could matter, and could eliminate a Classic from consideration.

The Cross Roads Classic LE was available in 2012, and the Classic was available in 2013 and 2014. The 2012 LE came one way: black paint, khaki accents, and red stripes, and as an LE, each unit also had a numbered plate. The list price was $17,999

The Cross Roads Classic had a list price of $17,999 in both 2013 and 2014. The 2013 model was burgundy and khaki with graphics, and the 2014 had two-tone Bronze Mist and khaki paint.

Model Name	Cross Roads Classic LE
Production Years	2012
Paint Colors	Black and Khaki With graphics

Model Name	Cross Roads Classic
Production Years	2013-2014
Paint Colors	See Appendix C: Cross Roads Classic

Note: *Refer to the Cross Roads for specifications. Note that a windshield and leather-look saddlebags were standard on each of these models.*

For 2014, the Classic's final year of production, the bike had a Two-Tone Bronze Mist & Khaki paint job and the same equipment as in 2013. The leather-looking saddlebags coordinated well with the bike's classic style, but they were not lockable. That was a distinct disadvantage compared to the roomy, lockable Cross Country bags. *Victory*

Here's the view from the seat of a 2014 Cross Roads Classic. No audio, but like every bike built on the versatile Cross-bike platform, it was a smooth-riding, easy-handling bike. *Victory*

Taste is subjective, but for a massive, fully equipped touring motorcycle, this is a beautiful bike. The fairing and front lowers combined to provide outstanding wind and weather protection, and the airflow was adjustable. The saddlebags were massive, as was the trunk, which could be installed and removed without tools. *Author*

Cross Country Tour

Just as the Kingpin was accessorized to become the Kingpin Tour, the Cross Country Tour was the fully decked-out evolution of the Cross Country.

Introduced in 2012 and popular until the brand's end, the Cross Country Tour was an outstanding bike for all types of cruising, from local to long, long distance. It had power, smooth handling, tremendous comfort, extensive electronic features, immense cargo space, and versatility.

Equipment that made the Tour a long-riding king included: the lowers mounted on the highway bars, heated handlebar grips and seats (with individual high-low heat controls for the passenger and driver), height-adjustable passenger footrests, front and rear tip-over protection, and the Lock & Ride trunk. As with Polaris's Lock & Ride equipment that was popular on the company's off-road vehicles, the trunk could be installed on or removed without tools. It locked onto the saddlebag brackets and an electrical connection powered the audio speakers, taillight in the trunk lid, and the interior charging outlet.

The bike also came with a tall touring windshield, which this book's author found troubling during rainy riding. Water beaded up on both sides of the

This concept created by Senior Staff Industrial Designer Mike Song shows a bike that's nearly identical to the production Cross Country Tour. The fuel tank and trunk look more swoopy and styled than the finished pieces, but most other components are true to what was built.

Mike Song

windshield—and it was an extremely large piece—making it difficult to look around the edge of the windshield to see the road. But it offered excellent wind protection in (dry) cold-weather riding.

Another feature that added comfort was the Victory Comfort Control System (a name that never gained traction among riders or dealers). This "system" included the fairing-mounted upper air controls and lowers-mounted bottom air vents that let a driver control airflow from the front end of the bike. In cold or wet weather, closed vents were highly effective at blocking the elements. In hot weather, open vents allowed airflow that swept away engine heat.

There was also a small cargo space (think: glove compartment) in each lower. Both cargo spaces were within reach of the driver, and were handy for holding gloves, snacks, and more. The left lower's cargo hold had a cord to connect devices such as iPods.

Victory correctly claimed that the Cross Country Tour offered more cargo space than any stock motorcycle in the world. The large saddlebags, huge trunk, and cargo boxes in the lowers provided a combined 41 gallons of cargo space, all of which was weather-protected. The trunk and bags were lockable, and accessory locks were available for the glove boxes.

Like the Cross Country, the Tour had anti-lock braking, cruise control, and an audio system in the fairing. Along with the two fairing speakers, the Tour had two forward-facing audio speakers in the trunk housing.

The base Cross Country was one of Victory's best bikes ever, and the touring equipment added to create the Tour enhanced long-riding opportunities. Your author completed multiple Iron Butt rides on Tours, and when discussing the bike with customers at rallies or bike shows, could recommend only one

This 2015 Cross Country Tour shows how the bike's style lines adroitly accommodate two-tone paint schemes. This bike sports a few non-stock accessories, including the black mirrors and the color-matched headlight bezel and LED headlight. *Victory*

accessory: a lower windshield. Other than that, the bike had everything a rider—or two—could need.

When it debuted for 2012, the base Cross Country Tour (solid black) had a U.S. MSRP of $21,999.

To celebrate the debut of the Tour, Victory hosted the World's Longest Test Ride (WLTR). A pair of Tours were ridden from coast to coast in relay fashion. Riding on each of the four legs were a Victory advocate and a consumer who owned another brand of bike. Victory chronicled the trip from the Arlen Ness dealership in Dublin, California, to Washington, D.C., on social media, and the non-Victory riders praised the Tour riding experience profusely along the way.

Model Name	Cross Country Tour
Production Years	2012–2017
Length	108.1 inches
Wheelbase	65.7 inches
Seat Height	26.25 inches
Ground Clearance	5.8 inches
Dry Weight	845 pounds
Engine	Victory 106-ci Freedom Engine
Exhaust	Split dual exhaust with crossover
Final Drive	Belt-drive
Fuel Capacity	5.8 U.S. gallons
Front Suspension	Inverted cartridge telescopic forks, 43mm diameter; 5.1 inches of travel
Front Brakes	Dual 300mm floating rotors with four-piston caliper; ABS
Rear Suspension	Single mono-tube gas shock, cast-aluminum swingarm with constant rate linkage; adjustable air spring; 4.7 inches of travel
Rear Brakes	300mm floating rotor with two-piston caliper
Front Wheel	18.0×3.0-inch cast-aluminum wheel
Rear Wheel	16.0×5.0-inch cast-aluminum wheel
Front Tire	130/70R18 Dunlop Elite 3
Rear Tire	180/60R16 Dunlop Elite 3
Frame	Cast-aluminum frame; uses the engine as a stressed member
Instrumentation	Analog speedometer and LCD that displays: tachometer, clock (time of day), gear position, diagnostic readouts, and warning lights; plus stand-alone fuel gauge
Lights	Twin-beam headlight, turn signals (front and rear), tail/brake light
Paint Colors	Black, Sunset Red, Pearl White (2012)

Cory Ness Signature Series Cross Country Tour

The Cross Country Tour was the base model for one Ness Signature Series bike: the 2013 Cory Ness model. It was Gold Digger Pearl with black Ness graphics, and was loaded with extras including: contrast billet wheels, Kicker premium audio speakers, a heated suede seat, and diamond-cut cylinders. The U.S. MSRP was $28,999.

Model Name	Cory Ness Signature Series Cross Country Tour
Production Years	2013
Paint Colors	Gold Digger Pearl With Black Ness Graphics

Note: *Same specifications as the standard Cross Country Tour except for the special features listed above.*

15th Anniversary Cross Country Tour

Victory introduced the 2014 15th Anniversary Cross Country Tour to celebrate the brand's anniversary. Only 150 of these limited-edition, numbered models were built. Each unit was a Cross Country Tour with special paint replicating the Antares Red and Black scheme of the first Victory ever built. It came with with special features including commemorative anniversary badges, chrome cargo racks for the saddlebags and trunk, trunk and saddlebag liners, fender trim, chrome sprocket cover, GPS, and XM Radio. Each one also had billet wheels, Kicker audio speakers, extra chrome, a custom seat with anniversary branding, and more. Unlike the 10th Anniversary Vision, the 15th anniversary bike did not have reverse. The U.S. MSRP was $29,999.

Model Name	15th Anniversary Cross Country Tour
Production Years	2014
Paint Colors	Sunset Red and Gloss Black with gold pinstriping

Note: *Same specifications as the standard Cross Country Tour except for the special features listed above.*

Magnum

In the marketing and advertising of all types of products, there's a lot of B.S. However, although Victory's marketing copy about the new 2015 Magnum sounded like hyperbole, it rang true: "Envy comes standard," was the Magnum tagline. "It's got a 21-inch wheel, slammed back-end, custom paint, and our best performing sound system ever—EVER!"

It was true: the Magnum had powerful appeal. Although good ol' traditional riders preferred the balanced ride of the standard Cross Country, the Magnum's style and seating position turned heads, planted rear ends in the seat, and sold bikes.

The Magnum started as a Cross Country, but was then tipped rearward with the combination of a stylish 21-inch front wheel and a lowered rear end

that Victory called "slammed." That might seem too strong for a bike lowered 1 inch in the rear through suspension re-engineering, but the effect was enhanced by the Low-Pro seat that lowered the rider farther. A Magnum rider felt like he was on a long-and-low custom. It was a bad-ass, "look at me" riding position that many Magnum owners took a step further with ape hangers or mini apes.

This tall-front/low-rear profile was just the start. A Magnum also had:

- Extensive custom-look paint, including a color-matched dashboard, headlight and taillight bezels, front radiator shroud, and saddlebag hardware

The Magnum's headlight and taillight bezels were color-matched, and the headlight output was powerful light provided by seven LED units. Victory claimed the headlight was 74 percent brighter than the standard Cross Country headlight.

Victory

- A wrap-around front fender that complemented the front wheel with a colorful arc of bodywork
- Color-matched close-out bodywork between the saddlebags and rear fender for a full-body custom look
- A low-profile Boomerang windshield
- Powerful LED lighting, front and rear
- A 100-watt audio system in the fairing

The head-turning 2015 Magnum retailed for $21,999 and came in the following paint schemes: Magnum Red Over Super Steel Gray; Plasma Lime With Silver; and Metasheen Black Over Super Steel Gray.

There was also a Ness model in Midnight Cherry with extensive Ness custom graphics for $22,999.

The 2016 model had the same list price as in 2015, and the '16 colors were: Black Crystal Over Super Steel Gray; Black Crystal Over Havasu Red; and Suede Pearl White With Black & Silver.

The final 2017 Magnums had paint schemes that featured vintage muscle car colors and stripes. The colors and prices were: Gloss Black With Graphics ($22,599); Habanero Inferno Orange With Graphics ($23,099); and Indy Red Pearl With Graphics ($23,099).

Model Name	Magnum
Production Years	2015–2017
Length	104.3 inches
Wheelbase	65.7 inches
Seat Height	26.3 inches
Ground Clearance	5.8 inches
Dry Weight	760 pounds
Engine	Victory 106-ci Freedom Engine
Exhaust	Split dual exhaust with crossover
Final Drive	Belt-drive
Fuel Capacity	5.8 U.S. gallons
Front Suspension	Inverted cartridge telescopic forks, 43mm diameter; 5.1 inches of travel
Front Brakes	Dual 300mm floating rotors with four-piston caliper; ABS
Rear Suspension	Single mono-tube gas shock, cast-aluminum swingarm with constant rate linkage; adjustable air spring; 4.7 inches of travel
Rear Brakes	300mm floating rotor with two-piston caliper
Front Wheel	21.0×3.5-inch wheel
Rear Wheel	16.0×5.0-inch wheel
Front Tire	120/70R21 Dunlop Elite 3
Rear Tire	180/60R16 Dunlop Elite 3
Frame	Cast-aluminum frame; uses the engine as a stressed member
Instrumentation	Analog speedometer and LCD that displays: tachometer, clock (time of day), gear position, diagnostic readouts, and warning lights; plus stand-alone fuel gauge
Lights	Twin-beam headlight, turn signals (front and rear), tail/brake light
Paint Colors	See Appendix C: Magnum

Ness Signature Series Magnum

The final Ness Signature Series model ever offered was the 2015 Ness Magnum, a bike with a flashy Midnight Cherry paint scheme with accents and graphics, and a few Ness accessories. It was an eye-catching bike, but a "standard" Magnum was so flamboyant that this Ness model did not stand apart the way many others had. The U.S. MSRP for this model was $22,999.

Model Name	Ness Magnum
Production Years	2015
Paint Colors	Ness Midnight Cherry With Ness Graphics

Note: *Refer to Magnum specifications for model details.*

The Magnum came with a 100-watt audio system that had six speakers in the fairing. The drive-facing dashboard was color-matched, not the flat black of a Cross Country. This bike had accessory ape hangers, which were probably the second-most popular accessory for a Magnum, right behind the Stage 1 exhaust. *Victory*

The Magnum had a 21-inch wheel (versus the Cross Country's 18-incher), and the rear end was, as Victory described it, "slammed." The rider sat lower on the Magnum and the shaved-out seat felt like a bucket with modest lower back support that riders loved. *Victory*

The first Magnum X-1 featured stunning custom-look paint and all the features of the Magnum, plus the saddlebag lid audio, which complemented the fairing audio with four more speakers and another 100 watts of audio power. The X-1 also had a smoke-tinted LED headlight and billet wheels. *Victory*

Magnum X-1

On Main Street at Daytona Bike Week 2015, Victory introduced the first Magnum X-1 model, a limited-edition Magnum. It had billet wheels, a distinctive paint scheme—Electric Red Over Gloss Black & Platinum—and saddlebag lid audio. This rear audio consisted of a pair of speakers in each bag lid and an amp to power the rear speakers, giving the bike a cumulative 10 speakers and 200 watts of premium audio.

Editors at Baggers.com said about the bike's audio: "The sound system can be compared to buying a semi-truck to tow a jet-ski, it's way overkill, and that's why it makes it so worth it."

The first X-1 had U.S. MSRP of $24,499. Victory introduced a new X-1 about every six months, and at Daytona Bike Week 2016, it unveiled the Magnum X-1 Stealth Edition, which featured an understated (for any Magnum) Stealth Gray paint job and sold for $23,499. The final Magnum X-1 Victory produced was a 2017 model with Pearl White with Platinum Overlay & Electric Red Pinstripes. The MSRP was $24,499.

Model Name	Magnum X-1
Production Years	2015–2017
Paint Colors	See Appendix C: Magnum X-1

X-1 models strutted down the street, showing off their 21-inch black billet wheels. The wheel was 3 inches taller than a stock Cross Country front wheel, yet Victory engineers made the necessary adjustments and the X-1 delivered the same outstanding handling as a Cross Country. *Victory*

The Magnum X-1 Stealth Edition was a striking departure from the original X-1. The Stealth model featured a monochrome look with its suede Stealth Gray paint. *Victory*

Victory spokesperson "The Gunny" liked the looks of the final X-1 package. Had Victory remained in operation, the Cross Country, Magnum, and Magnum X-1 would have remained lineup staples until a new Cross-bike-style platform was introduced. *Author*

CHAPTER 7

Victory Vision

The Victory Vision was big, bold, beloved, and definitely polarizing. It was Victory's first true, fully-equipped touring model, and it was positioned as direct competition for the best BMW, Gold Wing, or Harley-Davidson touring models. ("Victory Vision" was originally the official model name for the bike; "Victory" had to be included in the model name in the bike's early years to establish its trademark.)

The Vision was (and remains) an incredible motorcycle, one that its owners swore was the greatest two-wheeled machine ever to roll down the road. It was a bold step for Victory, but a few compromises kept it from ascending above all other touring bikes.

As Senior Staff Industrial Designer Mike Song recalled it, Victory began work on a flagship touring model in 2003. As the project moved forward and needed design attention, Song and Director of Industrial Design Greg Brew were swamped with other Polaris and Victory projects. Before joining Polaris, Brew had been director of transportation design for Designworks, a BMW Group design studio in Newbury Park, California. He knew from experience that they would be an ideal partner, and Designworks soon began the Vision styling work.

"We showed them some of my early concepts and we basically opened it up to them and their four or five designers," Song said of Designworks. "We gave them the pitch and let them go. They made the original concept model in four months and I flew out there every week for four months, making sure Greg's design direction was focused. I was more the design manager for that project. I designed the trunk and some smaller parts, and somebody from engineering came every other week."

The direction Victory gave was so informative, and Designworks produced such an impressive first concept, that the bike's styling changed minimally after that. "If you put the original painted mockup next to a production bike, there's almost no difference," Song said.

At the same time, a locked skunkworks was established deep inside the Polaris Product Development Center in Wyoming, Minnesota, for Victory engineers to work on the bike's hardware. Test mules were created and later trailered into the country under the cover of darkness for test runs on I-35. A group of bikes would ride with the black test bike (which

The Vision became not only the smoothest-riding Victory available, but also the most comfortable as features such as the front-end bodywork and electrically adjustable windshield provided outstanding rider protection.

Brian J. Nelson

NASCAR legend Richard Petty (on bike) and his son Kyle Petty helped introduce the Victory Vision models at the New York City IMS on January 19, 2007. The bikes—Vision Street and Vision Tour as shown here—were displayed at motorcycle shows and at Daytona Bike Week 2007. A special Vision demo tour let consumers ride the new bikes that summer. *Victory*

displayed fake branding) so that if any other motorists came close, the other riders could surround and block the view of the Vision mule.

The Vision represented the most complex plastic project Polaris had ever undertaken, and it had the company's most extensive electrical system and wiring harness to date. Development of the Vision was a major investment for Polaris—reportedly $22–24 million. Post-introduction investment on the bike was minimal, as the company waited, and waited, for sales to justify further product development.

Despite its high development costs, the Vision project proved invaluable to Victory. Product teams gained experience developing plastic bodywork and complex electronics, and it was the company's first bike with a two-piece cast-aluminum frame, a design that was adapted for the tremendously successful Cross bikes that followed the Vision to market. The

frame ran along the top of the bike, like the spine of an animal walking on all fours. On the Vision, the front frame piece served as the engine's air intake, with the air filter mounted at the open front of the piece. The frame design proved highly efficient—strong yet lightweight—and with no framework below the engine, bikes with this style of frame had outstanding cornering clearance.

Showtime in NYC

As development on the bike reached the final stages, Victory introduced the all-new Vision at the International Motorcycle Show (IMS) in New York City on January 19, 2007. NASCAR legend Richard Petty and his son Kyle Petty pulled the covers off a pair of bikes—a Vision Tour and Vision Street—to introduce the bikes that would be available later in the year as 2008 models.

The brown material is clay, and that's a full-sized clay model of the Vision in development at the Designworks studio in California. A real Freedom engine and actual front forks, wheel, and tire were used to ensure the positioning of these vital components. *Mike Song*

As expected—desired, in fact—the Vision was polarizing. It generated strong reactions, both good and bad, resulting in tremendous buzz and publicity for the model and the company. The bike's design was futuristic; one styling goal had been to integrate the side storage units into the bodywork, resulting in built-in compartments, rather than added-on saddlebags. The compartments were small—far smaller than an observer would expect from this large a bike with such expansive plastic bodywork. Because of this, Victory management made the call early in the NYC show to have the side storage compartments locked. However, the truly spacious trunk remained available for inspection and its cargo space did not disappoint.

Starting in New York and for years after, a common reaction to first seeing a Vision was to utter the name "Jetsons." Its design was that swoopy, non-traditional,

and futuristic. The Victory team correctly predicted that a significant segment of riders would hate the Vision, but that its distinctive style would also appeal to many, as would its long list of features. Many a loyal Vision owner, in fact, has reported at first being repulsed by the bike's looks, but being so impressed by its ride and handling that they bought the bike.

After the New York show, the Victory team finalized the bike's makeup and calibrations, and the first Vision rolled off the Spirit Lake assembly line on May 14, 2007. Then-Polaris CEO Tom Tiller climbed on the Supersteel Gray bike (which was still missing some bodywork) and put it through its post-assembly testing on the rolling dyno.

The Bike's Makeup

The Vision was presented as a luxury-touring model, and its equipment justified the label. (Originally,

This Vision rolling chassis is an incredible work of art. The engineering of the two-piece cast aluminum frame made the Vision a smooth-riding, great-handling bike, and a similar design worked just as well for the Cross bikes. The black vertical component to the left of the rear wheel is the air-adjustable shock housing. *Victory*

Vision models were available with a variety of equipment packages, which are detailed later. For this discussion, we'll include all features.)

The Vision Tour came with: a plush two-up seat (with foam that was 4 inches deep), separate seat heat controls for the driver and passenger (Hi/Off/Lo), heated handlebar grips, a large windshield that could be raised and lowered electronically, passenger floorboards, 14-inch-long driver floorboards, cruise control, and exceptional wind and weather protection from the front-end bodywork. The front face of the trunk had a cushioned passenger backrest and dual audio speakers to complement the two fairing-mounted speakers.

The Vision helped introduce the Freedom 106/6 drivetrain: a 106-ci V-twin engine and a six-speed transmission with sixth as overdrive. The engine delivered outstanding power and throttle response that instilled confidence while riding in traffic, even with a passenger and cargo on board. The power was complemented by reliable braking; the bike had linked anti-lock braking, the first ABS on any Victory model.

The Vision ride was smooth, too. The single rear shock was air-adjustable, so a rider could adjust the air pressure to suit the load (driver, passenger, and cargo) on the bike. This was the first Victory with such a rear suspension, and a similar version was used on the Cross-bike platform.

It's almost indescribable how easily the Vision handles for such a large bike—it's best just experienced for oneself. The 2008 Vision Tour had a listed dry weight of 849 pounds, but as a Victory engineer said, "as soon as it turns a wheel, it's like it loses 200 pounds." Plus, since the engine was mounted up to the cast-aluminum frame, there was no framework under the engine, which gave the Vision (along with the Cross bikes) the greatest cornering clearance of any Victory.

The Vision was the only bike in Victory history with a stock hydraulic clutch. Its audio system provided riders with AM/FM and weather radio, and the system could accept audio from a wide variety of devices, such as iPods or smart phones. One early Vision accessory was a six-disk CD player that could be installed in the trunk—where it took up about one-third of the available cargo space.

This overhead view shows how the Vision handlebars stretched back to give the driver an easy reach to the grips and controls. The frame's low point, where the two frame pieces are bolted together, creates the Vision's low seat height. The hose visible atop the back frame section is the air line for the rear suspension. *Victory*

The bike's electrical system and wiring harness were versatile and impressive. Along with the bike's extensive stock electronics, the wiring harness accommodated accessories such as GPS, CB radio, helmet communicators, audio devices, and electric heated gear.

The front of the bike featured a broad, frame-mounted fairing with adjacent bodywork that stretched down to the floorboards and back to the driver seat via a bridge, or console. At the rear, the side storage compartments created smooth-flowing lines that tapered to the tail of the bike, which hosted an immense "V" taillight. At the rear of Vision *Tour* models was a big trunk, which shared styling cues with the rest of the bike. Vision *Street* models had no trunk, and a color-matched panel covered the space where the trunk would have mounted behind the passenger seat.

This CAD image of the rear suspension shows how the air valve would mount inside the door of the left cargo compartment. The shock and spring were inside the yellow vertical cylinder. *Victory*

An Immense Investment

Victory introduced the Vision with the proclamation: "We're not rewriting American history. We're writing its future." Hopes were so high for the platform, and it was viewed internally as being so far advanced beyond the market competition that Victory considered making the Vision a separate product line. In this scenario, there would have been a separate dealer agreement for the Vision business, like the Lincoln line of Ford's luxury automobiles. Just as not every Ford dealer carries Lincoln, not every Victory dealer would have carried a Vision.

But saner heads prevailed. The Vision was sold as part of every Victory model lineup through the final model year, 2017, and the bike was nearly unchanged throughout its production life. The bike's available colors changed from year to year, but almost no components changed. In the final years of production, internal staff wrestled with this dilemma: "The bike's original tooling has produced far more parts than originally planned, and tolerances may suffer, so do we discontinue the Vision or invest in new tooling?" The brand's demise rendered the debate moot, but the odds seemed slim that there would have been a 2018 Vision.

The Vision was the most difficult Victory for the Spirit Lake crew to produce, but its engineering and manufacture were so superb that the model's performance and reliability records were outstanding.

Pricing reflected the Vision's waning market appeal. The U.S. MSRPs for 2008 models included Vision Street, $18,999; Vision Street Premium, $20,499; and Vision Tour Premium, $21,499. The Vision MSRP went as high as $23,699 in 2010, but once the Cross Country became Victory's top-selling touring model, the Vision's price dropped, and in its final year of production, 2017, the Vision Tour MSRP was $21,099.

Model Name	Victory Vision Tour
Production Years	2008–2017
Length	104.9 inches
Wheelbase	65.7 inches
Seat Height	26.5 inches
Ground Clearance	5.8 inches
Dry Weight	849 pounds (Vision Street: 809 pounds)
Engine	Victory 106-ci Freedom Engine
Exhaust	Split dual exhaust with crossover
Final Drive	Belt-drive
Fuel Capacity	6.0 U.S. gallons
Front Suspension	Conventional telescopic forks, 46mm diameter; 5.1 inches of travel
Front Brakes	Dual 300mm floating rotors with four-piston caliper; ABS
Rear Suspension	Single mono-tube gas shock, cast-aluminum swingarm with constant rate linkage; adjustable air spring; 4.7 inches of travel
Rear Brakes	300mm floating rotor with two-piston caliper
Front Wheel	18.0×3.0-inch cast-aluminum wheel
Rear Wheel	16.0×5.0-inch cast-aluminum wheel
Front Tire	130/70R18 Dunlop Elite 3
Rear Tire	180/60R16 Dunlop Elite 3
Frame	Cast-aluminum frame; uses the engine as a stressed member
Instrumentation	Analog speedometer and LCD that displays: tachometer, clock (time of day), gear position, diagnostic readouts, and warning lights; plus stand-alone fuel gauge
Lights	Twin-beam headlight, turn signals (front and rear), tail/brake light
Paint Colors	Black, Midnight Cherry, Supersteel Gray (2008)

Veteran Victory Iron Butt rider Steve "Rollin'" Rolland is shown at Prudhoe Bay, Alaska, where he completed the Ultimate Coast to Coast IB ride. His ride on the Vision 8-Ball had begun in Key West, Florida. Steve had a run-flat car tire on the rear, and a semi-knobby front tire. *Courtesy of Steve Rolland*

Model Variety

Originally, the bike was available in two models: the Vision Tour (with a trunk) and the Vision Street (no trunk, but otherwise identical to the Tour). Both were available in the first two model years (2008, 2009), then the Vision Street was discontinued.

In 2008 and 2009, there was a Vision Street and a Vision Street Premium, and three Tour models: Tour, Tour Comfort, and Tour Premium. Of those Street models, features exclusive to the Premium included the power windshield, heated grips and seats, and extra chrome. The Tour Comfort had the power windshield

and heated elements, while the Tour Premium had these features plus extra chrome and a powerful HID (High-Intensity Discharge) headlights.

If a rider purchased a Vision Street, a color-matched accessory trunk was nearly $2,000, which resulted in Street sales lagging dramatically behind those of the Tour. Since most riders purchased models with the Comfort or Premium packages, starting in 2010, Victory offered the single Vision equipment package with the full complement of comfort features and the trunk.

Because it was based on the Victory Vision Street, the 2009 Arlen Ness Signature Series model came without a trunk. The demand for a trunk was so prevalent that the standard Vision Street was only produced for two years; the Vision Tour, with the trunk, remained in production through model year 2017. *Lee Klancher*

Arlen Ness Signature Series Visions

The Arlen Ness Signature Series Victory Vision was available as a limited-edition model from 2009–2013. Each model featured custom paint created by Arlen Ness, additional chrome accessories, and a numbered plate with a facsimile of Arlen's signature. In true Ness fashion, the bike was lowered, partially through a shorter rear shock, but also by using a seat with less foam. The effect was a comfortable "bucket seat" for the driver that riders loved.

The 2009–2010 Ness models had no trunk, but the 2011–2013 models came with a trunk. For 2011 only, the word "Tour" was added to the model name to reflect the presence of the trunk.

In 2009, Laura Klock was the first person to make an official run on a Victory Vision during the BUB Motorcycle Speed Trials at the Bonneville Salt Flats. She made one run at 122 miles per hour and backed it up with a run of 120 miles per hour. *Klock Werks*

Victory Vision Tour 10th Anniversary Edition

For 2009, Victory celebrated its first decade on the road by producing 100 units of the Victory Vision Tour 10th Anniversary Edition. The bike was painted as close as possible to the first-ever Victory, a close replication of the Antares Red and Black scheme with gold pinstripes.

The anniversary model was loaded with chrome and had billet wheels and sprocket, special badging (including a numbered plate on the console), GPS, custom exhaust tips, XM Radio and CB intercom, custom seats, and more. Plus, it was the only Victory ever to have reverse as standard equipment. The bike had a U.S. MSRP of $28,999 and the 100 units sold out quickly.

Victory Vision 8-Ball

The Victory Vision 8-Ball was available in 2010 and 2011. These all-black models had no trunk, and ABS and some electronic features, such as the audio system, were deleted. The U.S. MSRP for both model years was $17,999.

CHAPTER 8

Concept Bikes

Victory created at least three concept bikes over the years and featured the bikes at events like the Sturgis rally or winter motorcycle shows. The engineers created an additional bike, the AXE, when they were still based in Osceola, Wisconsin. The AXE was not a true concept, but was a true parts bike, assembled from what was available around the shop. It was a runner and was informally displayed near the Victory demo ride site at Daytona Bike Week.

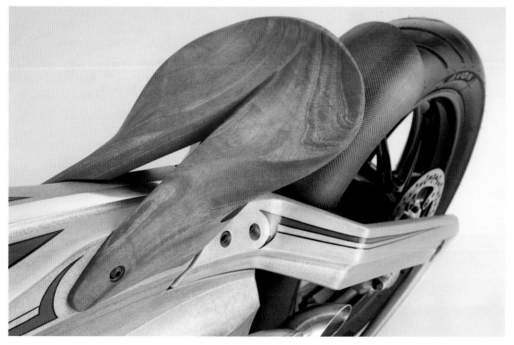

The CORE originally had an African mahogany seat. The fuel tank and frame featured pinstriping applied by Graphic Designer Steve Leszinski. *Victory*

Senior Staff Industrial Designer Mike Song posed with the CORE concept bike. The bike consisted of the barest essence of a motorcycle. *Author*

Visteon Vision Concept, 2001

Visteon, a Michigan-based automotive electronics company, approached Victory in 2000 with the idea of creating the Visteon Vision, a touring concept bike. The companies were already working together on the original Freedom engine, which was introduced in 2002 with a Visteon engine control unit (ECU).

The Visteon Vision Concept included a (real, or at least represented by switches) Visteon Fingerprint Identification System (replacing an ignition key); navigation system; Remote Lighting System, which used fiber optic cables to transmit light to both headlights; High-Intensity Discharge (HID) lighting and turn signals; Indirect Reflector Light Emitting Diode (LED) System; Visteon ECU, ignition coils, and leads; and heated seats and handlebar grips.

This concept had a styled fairing, lowers, and saddlebags, but not the extensive bodywork of the eventual production Vision. It had an original V92C engine and a gunslinger seat with a small passenger pad. The bike was displayed at the 2001 Sturgis rally.

The Visteon Vision concept bike looked remarkably similar to the Cross bikes that would not be produced for another decade. The bike featured a wide array of electronic controls that represented what Visteon could provide for use on the bike. *Victory*

Vision 800 Concept, 2005

The Victory Vision 800 concept made its debut—and re-introduced the Vision name—at the IMS in Long Beach, California, in December 2005. This Vision concept bike had: a single-sided (right side) swingarm, a CVT transmission like that of a Polaris ATV, and a low-slung 800cc parallel twin engine from a Polaris Sportsman 800 ATV.

The bike was originally shown with shaft drive, but was later converted to belt drive to make it more similar to other Victory models.

A fuel cell was positioned behind the front wheel, which freed up the top space—where a fuel tank would normally be positioned—for storage, with room enough for two full-faced helmets. The Vision 800 concept never entered production, but it was shown in numerous magazines worldwide and was featured in a Puma sportswear ad.

Industrial Designer Tiger Bracey sought to create a bike that was inviting and easy to ride for inexperienced riders. Many of the bike's mechanical elements are located under bodywork and out of sight. *Victory*

Senior Staff Industrial Designer Mike Song drew these concepts of the extremely spare CORE, and Greg Brew, Director of Industrial Design, insisted that the team build this fascinating bike. *Mike Song*

CORE Concept, 2009

The CORE concept bike was born high in the sky. Victory Industrial Designer Mike Song was on a flight home from a test-ride trip when he began drawing a raw, no-frills bobber. He recalled: "I thought, wouldn't it be cool to have a modern bobber, and use the cast frame of the Vision? I sketched it on the airplane, and when I got back to the office, hung it on my wall. [Director of Industrial Design] Greg Brew saw the sketch and he said, 'We gotta build that!'"

Song's in-flight sketch would become the foundation of the CORE concept bike.

The bike was little more than wheels, an engine, and a minimalist cast-aluminum frame. In a press release, Victory said the concept's name "perfectly reflects the essence of this concept motorcycle. It is, in fact, the raw 'core' or center of a motorcycle. There is no traditional bodywork; the motorcycle is effectively turned inside-out with its architecture completely exposed. It also accentuates the innovative frame

Using the CORE as a starting point, Mike Song expanded on the idea to develop concepts for a cruiser that could go into mass production. Elements of the Judge and Gunner are visible from these designs. *Mike Song*

The finished product was photographed on a frigid January afternoon in a north Minneapolis photo studio. A bikini-clad model from Florida, who was photographed with the bike, screamed when she had to lie next to it on the ice-cold concrete floor for an overhead photo. *Victory*

The finished CORE originally had an African mahogany seat and the fuel tank featured pinstriping applied by Graphic Designer Steve Leszinski. *Victory*

design and the process that is used to make the cast aluminum frame: the molten aluminum is poured into a sand core, which is removed when the casting process is complete."

Victory sand-cast two frames at a Minnesota foundry, and team members took turns with a sledge-hammer to break up the sand molds.

Song said the CORE was his inspiration for the Octane, but production and sales concerns forced his hand. If he had his way, the Octane would have had a tiny fuel tank like a true bobber. "A two-and-a-half-gallon fuel tank would have captured the form," he said.

Victory unveiled the CORE concept at the International Motorcycle Show in New York City in January 2009. The CORE was a runner, and the Industrial Design team brought it to Sturgis one year for some Badlands riding and photography.

Senior Staff Industrial Designer Mike Song evaluated the CORE's handlebar design and position. *Mike Song*

Former industrial design team member, Ryan Andreae (right), discussed assembly details of the CORE. *Victory*

A parts bike created by members of the Victory engineering team, The AXE was underappreciated and underpublicized. It was a raw, powerfully styled bike with daunting pointed tops on its solid forks. *Author*

AXE Concept

Before Victory engineering moved into the Polaris Product Development Center in Wyoming, Minnesota, the team was based in a Polaris facility in Osceola, Wisconsin. For fun, and to use some of their pent-up creativity, the team created "the AXE," a concept bike, if you will, made from available parts. Team members worked on it in their free time, and had an intern do much of the hands-on building. The bike had raw, powerful style, with minimal bodywork and solid forks with pointed tops. The bike was a runner and was displayed and ridden around Daytona Beach during Daytona Bike Week 2005.

Several members of the Victory engineering team posed with The AXE. In their free time, these men and others on the team, created the bike from spare parts. *Victory*

Victory Engines

Original Victory Engine (1998–2001)

Engine Type	Air/oil-cooled 50-degree V-twin
Bore × Stroke	97×102mm
Displacement	1,507cc (91.92 cubic inches)
Compression Ratio	8.5:1
Valvetrain	Single overhead cam; self-adjusting cam chains; 4 valves per cylinder; hydraulic lifters
Lubrication	Dry sump
Oil Capacity	6 quarts
Electrical Power	28 amps
Fuel System	Electronic Fuel Injection with 44mm throttle bores
Primary Drive	Gear drive with torque compensator
Clutch	Wet, multi-plate
Transmission	Five-speed

Victory 92-ci Freedom Engine (Introduced 2002)

Engine Type	Air/oil-cooled 50-degree V-twin
Bore × Stroke	97×102mm
Displacement	1,507cc (91.92 cubic inches)
Compression Ratio	9.2:1
Valvetrain	Single overhead cam; self-adjusting cam chains; 4 valves per cylinder; hydraulic lifters
Lubrication	Dry sump
Oil Capacity	6 quarts
Electrical Power	38 amps
Fuel System	Electronic Fuel Injection with 44mm throttle bores
Exhaust	Staggered dual exhaust
Primary Drive	Gear drive with torque compensator
Clutch	Wet, multi-plate
Transmission	Five-speed

Victory 100-ci Freedom Engine (Introduced 2005)

Engine Type	Air/oil-cooled 50-degree V-twin
Bore × Stroke	101×102mm
Displacement	1,634cc (99.7 cubic inches)
Compression Ratio	9.8:1
Valvetrain	Single overhead cam; self-adjusting cam chains; 4 valves per cylinder; hydraulic lifters

Victory 100-ci Freedom Engine (Introduced 2005) (cont.)

Lubrication	Dry sump
Oil Capacity	5 quarts
Electrical Power	38 amps
Fuel System	Electronic Fuel Injection with 44mm throttle bores
Primary Drive	Gear drive with torque compensator
Clutch	Wet, multi-plate
Transmission	Six-speed or Five-speed

Victory 106-ci Freedom Engine (Introduced 2008)

Engine Type	Air/oil-cooled 50-degree V-twin
Bore × Stroke	101×108mm
Displacement	1,731cc (106 cubic inches)
Compression Ratio	9.4:1
Valvetrain	Single overhead cam; self-adjusting cam chains; 4 valves per cylinder; hydraulic lifters
Lubrication	Dry sump
Oil Capacity	5 quarts
Electrical Power	50 amps
Fuel System	Electronic Fuel Injection with 45mm throttle bores
Primary Drive	Gear drive with torque compensator
Clutch	Wet, multi-plate
Transmission	Six-speed

Victory 1200-ci Octane Engine (Introduced 2016)

Engine Type	Liquid-cooled 60-degree V-twin
Bore × Stroke	101×73.6mm
Displacement	1,179cc
Compression Ratio	10.8:1
Valvetrain	Dual overhead cam; 4 valves per cylinder
Lubrication	Dry sump
Oil Capacity	5 quarts
Electrical Power	50 amps
Fuel System	Sequential fuel injection with single 60mm throttle body
Primary Drive	Gear drive with torque compensator
Clutch	Wet, multi-plate
Transmission	Six-speed

Racing and World Records

V92C Speed & Distance Rides

For a cruiser motorcycle brand, Victory had an impressive history of competitive feats. Victory riders even set a few world records. Joe Klein, then age 65, was the first Victory rider to post a speed on the Bonneville Salt Flats. During Speed Weeks in 2000, Joe ran 106 mph on a virtually stock V92SC. Laid out over the tank during his run, Joe said, "I started to get a little tank slapping out of it, but I said, 'Go for it! Go! Go!' It was great, and we were proud to put a Victory in the record books." In 1998, Joe was the first to ride a Victory (V92C) across the country on his "Rock to Rock" ride from New York City to San Francisco.

Speed Run Record Setters

Running as a privateer on a modified Kingpin, Gregor Moe set an AMA National Land Speed Record of 165.863 miles per hour in the 2000-M-AG class at the Bonneville Salt Flats on September 3, 2009. One year later, he rode the same bike to a new class record speed of 166.485 miles per hour. (Moe was also the first Victory rider to achieve Mile Eater Gold status from the Iron Butt Association for his 30-plus Iron Butt

Riding a modified 2008 Hammer on the Bonneville Salt Flats, Brian Klock set a speed record of 173.223 miles per hour in the M-BG-2000 class in August 2014. *Lloyd Greer*

rides.) At Bonneville in August 2014, Brian Klock set an M-BG-2000 class record of 173.223 miles per hour on a modified 2008 Hammer. The bike was built and prepped by Lloyd Greer and students from the Helping With Horsepower program he established to help at-risk high school students in Pine Bush, N.Y. Greer's Victory/Indian aftermarket performance shop, Lloyd'z Motorworkz, is also based in Pine Bush.

Isle of Man Podium Places

William Dunlop piloted an Empulse RR (listed as the Victory RR) to second place in the 2016 Isle of Man TT's SES TT Zero class for electric bikes. Dunlop ran his lap at an average speed of 115.844 miles per hour. In 2015, Lee Johnston finished third in the class with an average speed of 111.620 miles per hour on an Empulse RR, and Guy Martin took fourth (109.717 miles per hour).

Pikes Peak Hill Climb Success

At the 2015 Pikes Peak International Hill Climb, Don Canet (road test editor for *Cycle World* magazine) qualified fourth-best among motorcycles on

Gregor Moe ran as a privateer, self-funding his successful speed run effort. *Gregor Moe*

Racing on an Empulse RR (listed as the Victory RR), William Dunlop finished second in the 2016 Isle of Man TT's SES TT Zero class for electric bikes. He ran his lap at an average speed of 115.844 miles per hour. *Victory*

Don Canet takes a tight inside line through a corner while riding up Pikes Peak in the 2015 Hill Climb. *Author*

At the 2015 Pikes Peak International Hill Climb, Don Canet was fourth-fastest motorcycle qualifier on the Victory Project 156 bike, which was powered by a version of the engine that ended up in the Octane. *Victory*

the Victory Project 156 bike. The race bike built by Roland Sands Design was powered by a prototype Octane engine. Canet crashed in competition, resumed his run, but DNF'd as the bike quit just below the summit. In 2016, Canet won the electric bike class at Pikes Peak and posted the year's second-fastest motorcycle time on a Victory Empulse RR. Jeremy Toye raced the Project 156 bike that year and won the Exhibition Powersport class while posting the third-fastest motorcycle time.

On the Drag Strips

In 2011, Dave Koehmstedt made history by becoming the first Victory rider to win a national racing championship. Competing against Harley-Davidsons in the American Motorcycle Racing Association (AMRA), he won the 2011 Pro Eliminator class title. He also finished fourth in Eliminator and Modified points. Koehmstedt and Victory rider Mike "Jethro" Pearce competed in AMRA racing for several years. Victory sponsored Matt and Angie Smith as both raced in the NHRA's Pro Stock Motorcycle class in 2016. Their race bikes were labeled as Victory Gunners. Matt Smith won one final and finished sixth in points, while Angie finished 16th. In 2017, following the Victory wind-down announcement, Matt raced on a bike listed as a "Polaris Victory Magnum," while Angie ran on a Buell.

Matt Smith launches his NHRA Pro Stock Motorcycle bike down the strip. Victory sponsored Smith's race team in 2016, when Matt and his wife Angie raced on bikes labeled as Victory Gunners. *Victory*

Victory Record Setters

Victory Stunt Team rider Joe Dryden set the world record for the Longest Motorcycle Burnout on a 2017 Octane at Orlando Speed World on March 2, 2016. Dryden executed a continuous burnout measuring 2.23 miles (3.58 km) in length. He rode just over seven laps around the 3/8-mile oval track before the bike's rear tire disintegrated. Swiss endurance rider Urs "Grizzly" Pedraita set a world record in 2016 for the fastest circumnavigation of the world on a motorcycle. Riding a specially equipped Cross Country Tour, he crossed five continents, usually riding alone, in 119 days and 21 hours (including transport time between continents). He covered roughly 47,390 miles in 72 days and 13 hours of actual riding.

In March 2016, Victory Stunt Team rider Joe Dryden roasted a rear tire en route to a world record for the longest motorcycle burnout. *Victory*

Tony Carbajal showed how to conserve Octane front tire rubber. The Victory Stunt Team punished Octane rear fenders and taillights because the bikes were so easy for them to wheelie. *Victory*

Swiss endurance rider Urs "Grizzly" Pedraita rode a specially modified Cross Country when he set a world record in 2016 for the fastest circumnavigation of the world on a motorcycle. *Victory*

Victory Paint Colors by Year

V92C
1998–1999: Antares Red & Black With Gold Pinstripes; KYSO [Knock Your Socks Off] Blue & Black With Gold Pinstripes
2000: P.H.A.T. Black; Two-Tone P.H.A.T. Black/Steel Grey; Two-Tone Champion Red/P.H.A.T. Black
2001: P.H.A.T. Black; P.H.A.T. Black & Steel Grey; Midnight Blue & Cashmere Metallic
2002: Black; Solar Red & Pearl White; Speed Yellow & Black
2003: Black; Sonic Blue; Flame Yellow; Solar Red; Retro Turquoise & Stone White; Sonic Blue & Vogue Silver; Black With Hot Rod Flames; Solar Red & Vogue Silver; Flame Yellow & Black

V92C SE
1999: Candy Antares Red; P.H.A.T. Black

V92C Deluxe
2001: P.H.A.T. Black; Money Green & Cashmere Metallic; Vanilla Cream & Carmen Metallic
2002: Black; Solar Red & Pearl White; Sonic Blue & Pearl White; Cobalt Green & Pearl White; Speed Yellow & Black

V92SC/SportCruiser
2000: P.H.A.T. Black; Steel Grey; Champion Red
2001: P.H.A.T. Black; Steel Grey; Speed Yellow With White Racing Stripes

V92TC/Touring Cruiser
2002: Black; Sonic Blue & Vogue Silver; Solar Red & Vogue Silver
2003: Black; Sonic Blue; Solar Red; Cobalt Green & Champagne; Black With Hot Rod Flames; Sonic Blue & Champagne; Retro Turquoise & Stone White; Solar Red & Champagne; Black & Vogue Silver
2004: Black; Solar Red; Sonic Blue; Cobalt Green & Champagne; Bronze Mist & Pearl White; Black & Bronze Mist; Sonic Blue With Hot Rod Flames; Purple Thunder With Silver Hot Rod Flames
2005: Black; Solar Red; Sonic Blue; Pearl White Over Vogue Silver; Polaris 50th Anniversary Editions (Sonic Blue and Vogue Silver with gold accents); Black With Hot Rod Flames [COP only]
2006: Black; Two-Tone Sedona Over Stone Beige; Two-Tone Graphite Over Turbo Silver

V92TC Deluxe
2002: Black; Champagne & Pearl White; Black & Vogue Silver; Solar Red & Vogue Silver; Sonic Blue & Vogue Silver

Vegas
2003: Black; Solar Red; Flame Yellow; Vogue Silver; Sonic Blue
2004: Black; Solar Red; Sonic Blue; Vogue Silver; Solar Red & Vogue Silver; Cosmic Sunburst & Vogue Silver; Sonic Blue With Tribal Fade Flames; Purple Thunder With Vogue Silver Tribal Flames
2005: Black; Solar Red; Sonic Blue; Flame Yellow; Pearl White Over Vogue Silver; Polaris 50th Anniversary Editions (Sonic Blue and Vogue Silver with gold accents); Indy Red With Tribal Fade Flames; Black With Tribal Fade Flames
2006: Black; Indy Red; Supersonic Blue; Two-Tone Graphite Over Turbo Silver; Two-Tone Flame Yellow Over Turbo Silver; Black With Red Pinstripes; Nuclear Sunset With Silver Tribal Flames
2007: Black; Turbo Silver With Firemist Clear; Pearl White/Super Graphite; Boardwalk Blue/Pearl White; Nuclear Sunset With Black Pinstripe
2008: Black; Midnight Cherry; Supersteel Gray; Two-Tone Midnight Blue/Cruiser Black; Sunset Red With Flames
2009: Black; Blue Ice; Pearl White; Sunset Red; Two-Tone Midnight Cherry/Pearl White With Carbon Stripe; Two-Tone Blue Ice/Pearl White With Carbon Stripe
2010: Pearl White; Two-Tone Sunset Red & Pearl White
2011: Two-Tone Imperial Blue & Pearl White; Crimson
2012: Two-Tone Imperial Blue & Pearl White; Two-Tone Sunset Red & Pearl White
2016: Sunset Red
2017: Sunset Red

Vegas Low
2008: Black; Midnight Cherry; Boardwalk Blue
2009: Black; Blue Ice; Pearl White; Sunset Red; Two-Tone Midnight Cherry/Pearl White With Carbon Stripe; Two-Tone Blue Ice/Pearl White With Carbon Stripe

Vegas LE
2010: Fireball Red and Black With Graphics; Competition Yellow and Black with Graphics; Pearl White and Black With Graphics; Turbo Silver and Black With Graphics

Kingpin

2004: Black; Solar Red; Sonic Blue; Purple Thunder; Bronze Mist & Pearl White; Black & Bronze Mist; Sonic Blue With Tribal Fade Flames; Purple Thunder With Vogue Silver Tribal Flames

2005: Black; Solar Red; Sonic Blue; Black Over Vogue Silver; Pearl White Over Vogue Silver; Polaris 50th Anniversary Editions (Sonic Blue and Vogue Silver with gold accents); Pearl White With Vogue Silver Flames; Black With Tribal Fade Flames

2006: Black; Indy Red; Supersonic Blue; Silver Over Black With Cosmic Flames; Two-Tone Graphite Over Turbo Silver; Two-Tone Sedona Over Stone Beige; Pearl White Over Stone Beige With Cosmic Flames

2007: Solid Black; Turbo Silver With Firemist Clear; Super Graphite/Pearl White; Pearl White/Boardwalk Blue; Pearl White/Nuclear Sunset With Cosmic Flame

2008: Black; Midnight Cherry; Supersteel Gray; Two-Tone Sands Metallic/Black; Black With Flames

2009: Black; Blue Ice; Super Graphite; Two-Tone Blue Ice/Pearl White With Carbon Stripe; Two-Tone Midnight Cherry/Pearl White With Carbon Stripe

2010: Midnight Cherry; Two-Tone Ocean Blue & Sandstone Metallic

2011: Two-Tone Pearl White & Sandstone Metallic; Crimson

2012: Two-Tone Vogue Silver & Pearl White

Kingpin Low

2009: Black; Blue Ice; Super Graphite; Two-Tone Blue Ice/Pearl White With Carbon Stripe; Two-Tone Midnight Cherry/Pearl White With Carbon Stripe

Kingpin Deluxe

2005: Black; Solar Red; Sonic Blue; Black Over Vogue Silver; Pearl White Over Vogue Silver; Pearl White With Vogue Silver Flames; Black With Tribal Fade Flames

2006: Black; Indy Red; Supersonic Blue; Silver Over Black With Cosmic Flames; Two-Tone Graphite Over Turbo Silver; Two-Tone Sedona Over Stone Beige; Pearl White Over Stone Beige With Cosmic Flames

Kingpin Tour

2007: Black; Turbo Silver With Firemist Clear; Super Graphite/Pearl White; Pearl White/Boardwalk Blue

2008: Black; Midnight Cherry; Supersteel Gray; Two-Tone Sands Metallic/Black; Black With Flames

2009: Black; Blue Ice; Super Graphite; Two-Tone Blue Ice/Pearl White With Carbon Stripe; Two-Tone Midnight Cherry/Pearl White With Carbon Stripe

Hammer

2005: Black; Indy Red; Cosmic Sunburst; Flame Yellow; Indy Red With Tribal Tattoo; Toxic Green With Tribal Tattoo [COP only]

2006: Black; Indy Red; Supersonic Blue; Nuclear Sunset With Tribal Tattoo Graphics; Flame Yellow With Tribal Tattoo Graphics

2007: Black; Turbo Silver With Firemist Clear; Solid Nuclear Sunset

2008: Black; Midnight Cherry; Supersteel Gray; Boardwalk Blue

2009: Black; Super Graphite; Sunset Red With Extreme Graphics; Nuclear Sunset With Extreme Graphics

2010: Blue Ice With Extreme Graphics

2011: Imperial Blue Metallic

Hammer S

2007: Sunset Red/Black

2008: Black With Turbo Silver Racing Stripes

2009: Boardwalk Blue With White Racing Stripes

2010: Suede Black & White With Red Stripe; Boardwalk Blue With White Racing Stripes

2011: Suede Black & Red With White Stripe

2012: Fireball Red & White Lightning With Graphics; Suede Black & Indy Red

2016: Gloss Black With Red Racing Stripes

2017: Gloss Black With White Racing Stripes

Vegas Jackpot

2006: Black; Sunset Red; Competition Yellow With Extreme Graphics; Sunset Red With Extreme Graphics; Black With Extreme Graphics (COP only)

2007: Black; Orange Crush; Sunset Red; Sunset Red With Extreme Graphics; Competition Yellow With Extreme Graphics; Pearl White With Extreme Graphics

2008: Black; Midnight Cherry; Boardwalk Blue; Two-Tone Black & Silver With Graphics; Two-Tone Black & Red With Graphics

2009: Black; Boardwalk Blue; Sunset Red; Orange Crush With Extreme Graphics; Lucky Lime With Extreme Graphics

2010: Black; Tequila Gold With Extreme Graphics

2011: Black; Pearl White & Black With Extreme Graphics; Black & Indy Red With Extreme Graphics

2012: Black; Pearl White & Black With Extreme Graphics; Fireball Red With White Scallops

2013: Orange Madness With Graphics

2014: Sunset Red & Gloss Black

High-Ball

2012: Suede Black With White & Graphics

2013: Suede Black With White

2014: Suede Black & White; Suede Black With Flames

2015: Suede Black With Silver Pinstripes

2016: Suede Black With White Tank Graphic

2017: Suede Black; Suede Nuclear Sunset Orange

Judge

2013: Gloss Black; Gloss Sunset Red; Suede Nuclear Sunset [Matte Orange]

2014: Gloss Black; Havasu Red

Boardwalk

2013: Gloss Black; Pearl White

2014: Two-Tone Sunset Red & Gloss Black

Gunner

2014: Suede Titanium Metallic With Graphics
2015: Suede Titanium Metallic With Graphics; Suede Green Metallic With Graphics
2016: Suede Titanium Metallic With Black Tank Graphics; Suede Green Metallic With Black Tank Graphics
2017: Suede Titanium Metallic; Suede Sagebrush Green Metallic

Octane

2016: Matte Super Steel Gray
2017: Gloss Black; Matte Super Steel Gray; Suede Pearl White; Gloss Black With Graphics

Empulse TT

2016: Titanium Silver & Havasu Red
2017: Titanium Silver & Havasu Red

Cross Roads

2010: Black; Midnight Cherry
2011: Black; Crimson
2012: Black; Sunset Red

Cross Roads Classic LE

2012: Black & Khaki With Graphics

Cross Roads Classic

2013: Burgundy & Khaki With Graphics
2014: Two-Tone Bronze Mist & Khaki With Pinstripes

Victory Hard-Ball

2013: Matte Black With Red Pinstripes

Cross Country

2010: Black; Midnight Cherry; Black & Graphite With Extreme Skulls
2011: Black; Imperial Blue Metallic; Two-Tone Pearl White & Vogue Silver
2012: Black; Imperial Blue; Two-Tone Sunset Red & Silver Graphics
2013: Gloss Black; Suede Nuclear Sunset (Blacked Out); Sunset Red (Blacked Out); Anti-Freeze Green With Black Flame; Midnight Metallic Flame and Black Gloss
2014: Gloss Black; Havasu Red; White Metallic; Suede Titanium Metallic; Two-Tone Boss Blue & Gloss Black; Two-Tone Suede Supersteel & Black; Suede Silver With Flames; Tequila Gold With Flames
2015: Suede White Frost; Suede Titanium Metallic; Gloss Titanium Metallic; Suede Black With Red Pinstripes; Havasu Red With Black Flames; Two-Tone Suede Sunset Red Over Black
2016: Suede Pearl White; Suede Titanium Metallic; Havasu Red Pearl
2017: Gloss Black; Suede White Frost; Suede Nuclear Sunset Orange; Sunset Red

Magnum

2015: Metasheen Black Over Super Steel Gray; Magnum Red Over Super Steel Gray; Plasma Lime With Silver
2016: Black Crystal Over Super Steel Gray; Black Crystal Over Havasu Red; Suede Pearl White With Black & Silver
2017: Gloss Black With Graphics; Habanero Inferno Orange With Graphics; Indy Red Pearl With Graphics

Magnum X-1

2015: Electric Red Over Gloss Black & Platinum
2016: Stealth Gray
2017: Pearl White With Platinum Overlay & Electric Red Pinstripes

Victory Vision Street

2008: Black; Midnight Cherry; Supersteel Gray
2009: Black; Midnight Cherry; Blue Ice

Victory Vision Tour

2008: Black; Midnight Cherry; Supersteel Gray
2009: Black; Midnight Cherry; Blue Ice
2010: Black; Pearl White; Two-Tone Ocean Blue & Sandstone Metallic
2011: Crimson & Black; Two-Tone Vogue Silver & Black; Pearl White
2012: Sunset Red & Black With Black Carbon Graphics; Imperial Blue & Supersteel Gray; Bronze Mist & Sandstone Metallic
2013: Black; Sunset Red & Black With Black Carbon Graphics; Bronze Mist & Sandstone Metallic
2014: Gloss Black; White Metallic; Nuclear Sunset Orange With Graphics
2015: Gloss Black; Sunset Red With Black Pinstripes
2016: Gloss Black; Blue Fire Gloss
2017: Gloss Black; Gloss Blue Fire

10th Anniversary Victory Vision

2009: Antares Red With Black Accents & Gold Pinstripes

Cross Country Tour

2012: Black; Pearl White; Sunset Red
2013: Gloss Black; Boardwalk Blue; Gold Mist; Solid Sunset Red
2014: Gloss Black; Two-Tone Sonic Blue & Silver; Two-Tone Gold Rush & Black
2015: Gloss Black; Two-Tone Havasu Red Pearl & Black; Two-Tone White Pearl & Gray
2016: Gloss Black; Gloss Pearl White With Supersteel Gray
2017: Gloss Black; Gloss Blue Fire; Two-Tone Turbo Silver & Black

15th Anniversary Victory Cross Country Tour

2014: Sunset Red and Gloss Black with Gold Pinstriping

8-Ball Models

Vegas 8-Ball
2005–2017: Gloss Black

Kingpin 8-Ball
2008–2011: Gloss Black

Hammer 8-Ball
2010–2015: Gloss Black

Vision 8-Ball
2010–2011: Gloss Black

Cross Roads 8-Ball
2014: Gloss Black

Cross Country 8-Ball
2014–2016: Gloss Black

Ness Signature Series Models

2004 Arlen Ness Signature Series Vegas
Custom Black Cherry Fade Paint

2005 Arlen Ness Signature Series Kingpin
"Purple Haze" Paint Scheme

2005 Cory Ness Signature Series Vegas
"Black & Blue" Paint Scheme

2006 Arlen Ness Signature Series Vegas Jackpot
Supersonic Blue With Arlen Ness Custom Graphics

2006 Cory Ness Signature Series Vegas Jackpot
Black With Arlen Ness Custom Graphics

2007 Arlen Ness Signature Series Vegas Jackpot
Black With Arlen Ness Custom Graphics

2007 Cory Ness Signature Series Vegas Jackpot
Silver With Cory Ness Custom Graphics

2008 Arlen Ness Signature Series Vegas Jackpot
Sunset Red With Arlen Ness Graphics

2008 Cory Ness Signature Series Vegas Jackpot
Metallic Purple With Cory Ness Graphics

2009 Arlen Ness Victory Vision
Black With Ness Custom Graphics

2009 Cory Ness Vegas Jackpot
Pearl White With Custom Ness Graphics

2010 Arlen Ness Vision
Black With Ness Custom Graphics

2010 Cory Ness Jackpot
Red With Ness Custom Graphics

2011 Arlen Ness Victory Vision
Black With Ness Graphics

2011 Cory Ness Cross Country
Sunset Red With Ness Graphics

2011 Zach Ness Vegas
Matte Black With Ness Graphics

2012 Arlen Ness Signature Series Victory Vision
Nuclear Sunset With Ness Graphics

2012 Cory Ness Signature Series Cross Country
Boardwalk Blue With Ness Graphics

2012 Zach Ness Signature Series Vegas 8-Ball
Titanium Metallic With Ness Graphics

2013 Arlen Ness Victory Vision
Havasu Red With Ness Graphics

2013 Cory Ness Cross Country Tour
Gold Digger Pearl With Ness Graphics

2013 Zach Ness Victory Cross Country
Suede Titanium Metallic

2014 Ness Cross Country
Havasu Red With Ness Custom Graphics

2015 Ness Magnum
Ness Midnight Cherry With Ness Graphics

Model List

Acknowledgments

A sincere thanks to the original Victory team, led by GM Matt Parks and Engineering Manager Geoff Burgess, and special Polaris contributors to the brand's launch and the original book: Bob Nygaard, Leanne (Koivisto) Peterson, Nancy Krenz, and Marlys Knutson. Also supporting the original book project were Wayne Davis, Jerry Hatfield, Henry Fiola, and Max Allers.

Too many great people fueled Victory's history to list, but among those who helped make this book possible are: Kara Nelson, Emily Norman, Savannah George, Emily Nemecek, Greg Pierce, Kris Jarland, Scott Jarland, Jack Herren, Bob Von Vett, Greg Richards, and Mike Song. A hat tip to Victory riders who provided resources, including Chuck Small, Mike Enright, Christopher Edwards, Richard Fowler, and Bill Toninato.

And special thanks to a supportive home team: Stela, Julia, Grace, and Sonja Dapper.
—MD

First and foremost, thanks to the folks at Victory. They took time to answer questions and dig up images when they were already working 14-hour days and made motorcycles available for photographs when the bikes needed to be elsewhere. It was a genuine pleasure to work with the Victory people; their cooperation and open-mindedness created an essentially uncut view of the creation of the V92C.

In addition to the Victory members mentioned by Mike Dapper, I'd like to thank Cory McWhorter, Scott Dieltz, Dave Muckenhern, Mike Benoy, Mike Danielson, Chuck Crone, Al Regelstad, Dewey Voss, Marshall Tennerman, Jay Schilling, Tom Neil and the rest of the Spirit Lake crew. A special thanks to Victory staffers Mark Bader, Steve Weinzerl, and Jennifer Rud who made extra efforts to help make this book.

Thanks are due to chase truck driver Michael Haenggi, fellow Motorbooks staff member Bob Wilson, and the folks at Motorbooks for making this all possible. Thanks to Dave Barley and the guys at Polar Aviation.

Thanks are also due to Michael Martinez for bringing his beautiful bike into Austin for a cover shoot.
—LK

Index